Before the Gospels

The Gospels of Thomas, Q, Signs, and The Passion:

The Writings from which the Gospels Sprang

by Joseph Lumpkin

Before the Gospels

Before The Gospels

Copyright © 2014 by Joseph Lumpkin

All rights reserved.

Printed in the United States of America. No part of this book may be used or reproduced in any manner whatsoever without written permission except in the case of brief quotations embodied in critical articles and reviews.

Fifth Estate Publishing, Blountsville, AL 35031

Cover Designed by An Quigley

Printed on acid-free paper

Library of Congress Control No: 2014935932

ISBN: 9781936533411

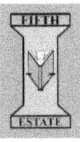

Fifth Estate, 2014

Table of Contents

Introduction	7
The Sayings Gospel or the Lost Gospel of Q	9
The Gospel of Thomas	75
The Passion Narrative	138
Mark	159
Matthew	164
Luke	169
John	178
The Signs Gospel	182
Conclusion	211
Appendix – Dating Ancient Manuscripts	228

Introduction

Jesus was a man of few words, simple words, and a deeply challenging message. However, through the years his words and message have been clouded with additions and redactions. How can we possibly know the words he spoke? What were his original teachings? Where did his message stop and the many changes begin? Hidden in the gospels themselves are the source materials containing the original message preached by Jesus.

Before the gospels were written, there were proto-gospels, notes, lists and collections used to construct the gospels we have today. Some gospels were used and built upon to form other, expanded gospels. **The "Q" Document** was used as a memory tool and literary scaffolding by Matthew and Luke in the writing of their gospels. Although many scholars believe Mark had access to the oldest parts of Q, others believe he did not. Since Mark predates Matthew and Luke they believe Mark was used as a template for Matthew and Luke. This would mean that Matthew started with Mark and added the Q sayings missing from Mark, along with Matthew's own stories, which is why Matthew seems to be simply an expansion of Mark's gospel. Of all the theories, the most accepted is the two source hypothesis, which maintains that Mark did not use Q but Matthew and Luke used both Q and Mark as their source materials.

The existence of a document containing a catalog of sayings was just a theory until the discovery of the **Gospel of Thomas.** Thomas is not Q, but is similar to Q in that it is an early repository of sayings of Jesus. Thomas and Q appear to be documents composed by people who followed Jesus and recorded his words. The Gospel of Thomas is a collection of 114 saying attributed directly to Jesus and proved the existence of a source material, which scholars believed explained why the wording of the synoptic gospels of Matthew, Mark, and Luke were so similar.

Mark also used a document called the **Passion Narrative** to establish a chronology and form the story of the crucifixion of Jesus. Since Matthew and Luke used Mark as a second source, the passion narrative occurs in their gospels also.

The gospel of John used a different source, called the **Signs Gospel**, which explains why it is so different to Mark, Matthew, and Luke. We will examine the writings behind the gospels. If the Christian faith is built upon the four gospels of Matthew, Mark, Luke, and John, then the underpinning documents, called "Q Gospel", Signs Gospel", and "Passion Narrative" are the foundation upon which these four gospels were based. They are the gospels behind the gospels and predate everything in the New Testament. They are the foundation stones of the faith upon which the four pillars of the gospels are built.

The Sayings Gospel or The Lost Gospel of Q

The Two-source hypothesis (or 2SH) is an explanation for the synoptic problem, which is the pattern of similarities and differences between the three Gospels of Matthew, Mark, and Luke. It posits that the Gospel of Matthew and the Gospel of Luke were based on the Gospel of Mark and a hypothetical sayings collection originating from the Christian Oral Tradition called Q. For the Two-source theory to work Q had to actually be a written document by the time it was used. The designation or name "Q" derives from the German word "Quelle," which means "Source."

Imagine, if you will, the child's game of "telephone" or "gossip" where the first person in a line of ten people tells the person in front of him or her a story and the person who has just heard the story tells it in turn to the next person, and so on until it gets to the tenth person, who tells the story aloud and compares it to the original story. The changes to the story are amazing and the two versions are barely noticeable as the same tale. This is how the gospels would have been dissimilar if Q had remained an oral tradition. Instead, Matthew and Luke are much more similar than not, proving both drew from at least one written source along the way.

Another view leading to the belief of a single written source can be seen every day in eyewitness events and reports. If two people, in this case Matthew and Luke, were to witness a single event and write about it, the wording of the stories and the details would vary greatly. Their vantage point, vocabulary, personalities, preferences, educations, writing styles, and other factors would allow the stories to diverge greatly. However, if they drew from the same single written source, relying on it as a base on their story, the two gospels would be very close. That is what we see demonstrated in the synoptic gospels. What variations do occur can be traced back to translation differences if Q had been written in Aramaic and Matthew and Luke written in Greek. The reason we expect Q to be in a written form is seen in the similarity of wording between Matthew and Luke with slight differences tracked back to Greek synonyms of Aramaic words.

The Gospel of Mark is usually dated between 60 and 100 A.D. Given the time that passed from the writing of the gospels, historical data proving or disproving the authenticity and authorship of the gospels are lacking, but we do have the following very obscure witness.

In the first half of the second century, Papias, a bishop of Hierapolis, wrote a five volume treatise called An Exposition of the Lord's Oracles. This book was in part a collection of oral folklore about early Christianity. Papias would ask people of age what they remembered about the formative years of the church. Eusebius commented on the writings of Papias, and on Papias himself, calling him a man of low intelligence and correcting ideas Papias had, which Eusebias claimed came from misinterpreting information from his interviews. Although this work is now lost, isolated fragments have been preserved in quotations and references by Irenaeus (c. 185), Eusebius (c. 300), and others. The following fragments relate to Papias's testimony on the authorship of the gospels:

14And in his own writing he [Papias] also hands down other accounts of the aforementioned Aristion of the words of the Lord and the traditions of the presbyter John, to which we refer those truly interested. Of necessity, we will now add to his reports set forth above a tradition about Mark who wrote the gospel, which he set forth as follows:

15And the presbyter would say this: Mark, who had indeed been Peter's interpreter, accurately wrote as much as he remembered, yet not in order, about that which was either said or did by the Lord. For he neither heard the Lord nor followed him, but later, as I said, Peter, who would make the teachings anecdotally but not exactly an arrangement of the Lord's reports, so that Mark did not fail by writing certain things as he recalled. For he had one purpose, not to omit what he heard or falsify them.

16Now this is reported by Papias about Mark, but about Matthew this was said, Now Matthew compiled the reports in a Hebrew manner of speech, but each interpreted them as he could.

17He himself used testimonies from the first epistle of John and similarly from that of Peter, and had also set forth another story about a woman who was accused of many sins before the Lord, which the Gospel according to the Hebrews contains. And let these things of necessity be brought to our attention in reference to what has been set forth.

So, Mark wrote down what Peter said about the life of Jesus, but it was not recorded in order, that is to say, chronologically at first.

Mark was probably written between 70 and 74 A.D. since he is writing to an audience that witnessed the destruction of the temple and takes that act as a sign of the coming apocalypse.

Modern scholars have advanced numerous elaborations and variations on the basic hypothesis of the source materials used to construct Mark, and even completely alternative hypotheses. Nevertheless, the Two-source hypothesis is supported by most biblical critics from all continents and most denominations.

Since the Q document has been lost, we can reconstruct it by using the "double tradition" material, that which is present in both

Matthew and Luke but not Mark. However, Q may also contain material that is preserved only by Matthew or only by Luke as well as material that is paralleled in Mark (called Mark/Q overlaps). The Mark overlap has led some to speculate that Mark had access to Q also, or at least parts of it.

Although the temptation story and the healing of the centurion's son are usually ascribed to Q, the majority of the Q material consists of sayings. For this reason, Q is sometimes called the Synoptic Sayings Source or the Sayings Gospel. Some scholars have observed that the Gospel of Thomas and the Q material, as contrasted with the four canonical gospels, are similar in their emphasis on the sayings of Jesus instead of the passion of Jesus.

Arguments in favor of the Two Source hypothesis state that Q can be discerned once Matthew's personal addition of collected and related materials are discounted.

C. M. Tuckett believes that variations between Matthew and Luke are due to variant translations of an Aramaic Q. It is doubtful if more than a very few cases of variation between Matthew and Luke can be explained in this way. Many of the alleged translation variants turn out to be simply cases of synonyms, and the differences between Matthew and Luke can often be explained just as well are due to the fact that two evangelists are telling the story in their own individual ways, one leaving out a story and substituting another. However, when the same source is used verbiage is so similar that it must have come from a common source.

Udo Schnelle comments in his book, *The History and Theology of the New Testament Writings,* The Sayings Source presumably originated in (north) *Palestine,* since its theological perspective is directed primarily to Israel. The proclamations of judgment at the beginning and end of the document are directed against Israel . The bearers of the Q tradition understand themselves to be faithful to the Law.

In the book *Ancient Christian Gospels,* **Helmut Koesterm points out that** the coming judgment explicitly in Q is written with the view to two Galilean towns, Chorazin and Bethsaida: even Tyre and Sidon will be better off in the coming judgment. These are the only names of places which occur in Q, besides a mention of John the Baptist's story in Jordan. It is, therefore, tempting to assume that the redaction of Q took place somewhere in Galilee and that the document as a whole reflects the experience of a Galilean community of followers of Jesus.

Even the sayings used for the original composition of Q were known and used elsewhere at an early date. They were known to Paul and were used in Corinth by his opponents. They existed in eastern Syria and were bases for the composition of the *Gospel of Thomas.* They were quoted by *1 Clement* in Rome at the end of the 1st century. The document itself, in its final redacted form, was used for the composition of Matthew and Luke, which both originated in the Greek-speaking church outside of Palestine. Thus, it is possible the Gospel of Thomas is a non-redacted and earlier form, which shows a fuller and more accurate representation of the sayings of Jesus. This is important to note. Helmut Koesterm and many other scholars mention redactions to Q.

(New Oxford American Dictionary)
redaction | ri'dak sh ən |
noun
the process of editing text for publication.
• a version of a text, such as a new edition or an abridged version.

Q, that is the "original" Q, was being changed, added to, edited, abridged, and was morphing, along with the evolution of the beliefs and doctrines of the faith itself. In other words, the original Q, and thus the portal through which to see the original words and deeds of Jesus, was being swept away. As the faith was being altered, so was Q. The Gospel of Thomas was being added to also, but not nearly with the speed and distortion of Q.

Udo Schnelle attempts to date Q by observing, "The Sayings Source was composed before the destruction of the temple, since the sayings against Jerusalem and the temple in Luke 13.34-35Q do not presuppose any military events. …The positive references to Gentiles in Q (cf. Luke 10.13-15Q; Luke 11.29-31Q; Matt. 8.5-13 Q; Matt. 5.47 Q; Matt. 22.1-10 Q) indicate that the Gentile mission had begun, which is probably to be located in the period between 40 and 50 AD."

Burton Mack states, "Mark wrote his story of Jesus some time after the war and shortly after Q had been revised with the Q additions. If we date Q around 75 C.E. to give some time for the additions obviously prompted by the war, Mark can be dated between 75 and 80 C.E. . . . For Mark, Q was extremely useful, for it had already positioned Jesus at the hinge of an epic-apocalyptic history, and it contained themes and narrative material that could easily be turned into a more eventful depiction of Jesus' public appearance. Q provided Mark with a large number of themes essential to his narrative. "

Mack continues: "Q also provided material that could easily be turned to advantage as building blocks in a coherent narrative account. The John-Jesus material was a great opener. The figure of the Holy Spirit was ready-made to connect the Q material in John and Jesus with the miracle stories Mark would use. Q's characterization of Jesus as the all-knowing one could be used to enhance his authority as a self-referential speaker in the pronouncement stories Mark already had from his own community. The notion of Jesus as the son of God could be used to create mystique, divide the house on the question of Jesus' true identity, and develop narrative anticipation, the device many scholars call Mark's "messianic secret." The apocalyptic predictions at the end of Q could then become instructions to the disciples at that point in the story where Jesus turns to go to Jerusalem. And, as scholars know, there are a myriad of interesting points at which the so-called overlaps between Mark and Q show Mark's use of Q material for his own narrative designs."

It is likely the trouble encountered in the dating of Q is due in part from various redactions and additions within Q. One theory presents three stages of development of the document. Although the elements would have occurred over a relatively short period of time, say 30 years, they can be seen in the following breakdown.

"Q1" - Describing Jesus as a Philosopher - Teacher

Prior to the writing of Q1, the Gospel message was passed verbally among individuals and groups. About 50 AD, or about twenty years after the death of Jesus, this oral tradition was written down. Thus, Q1 may be the truest report of Jesus' sayings. We will refer to it as Q1. The topics covered by Q1 are:

- who will belong to the "Kingdom of God"
- treating others (the Ethic of Reciprocity; a.k.a. Golden Rule)
- do not judge others
- working for the Kingdom
- asking for God's help
- do not fear speaking out
- don't worry about food, clothing, possessions

Before the Gospels

- the Kingdom will soon arrive
- the cost of being a follower
- the cost of rejecting the message

In a 2005 article, B.A. Robinson states, "What is remarkable about Q1 is that the original Christians appeared to be centered totally on concerns about their relationships with God and with other people, and their preparation for the imminent arrival of Kingdom of God on earth. Totally absent from their spiritual life are almost all of the factors that we associate with Christianity today. There is absolutely no mention of (in alphabetic order): adultery, angels, apostles, baptism, church, clergy, confirmation, crucifixion, demons, disciples, divorce, Eucharist, great commission to convert the world, healing, heaven, hell, incarnation, infancy stories, John the Baptist, Last Supper, life after death, Mary and Joseph and the rest of Jesus' family, magi, miracles, Jewish laws concerning behavior, marriage, Messiah, restrictions on sexual behavior, resurrection, roles of men and women, Sabbath, salvation, Satan, second coming, signs of the end of the age, sin, speaking in tongues, temple, tomb, transfiguration, trial of Jesus, trinity, or the virgin birth.

Jesus is described as a believer in God, but there are no indications that he was considered more than a gifted human being. His role was not as a Messiah or Lord but philosopher-teacher. The Gospel contains strong statements which are anti-family and which oppose Jewish religious rules. Rewards and punishments are described as occurring in this life, not after death. The "Kingdom of God" is

described as a type of utopian society on earth which his followers were creating, not some future location in heaven after death. God is presented as a loving father with an intimate concern for the welfare of believers. The Holy Spirit is mentioned, but appears as a gift given by God, not as a separate person of the Trinity. There is no reference to Jesus' death having any redeeming function; in fact, there is no mention of the crucifixion or resurrection at all."
Jesus was preaching a social message.

Some authors identify the contents of Q by numbering the sayings QS1 to QS64. Using this identification system, the Q1 material can be found at the following locations in the Gospel of Luke:

Q Location	Luke Location	Comments
QS7	6:20a	Start of the Beatitudes
QS8	6:20b-23	
QS9	6:27-35	
QS10	6:36-38	
QS11	6:39-40	
QS12	6:41-42	
QS13	6:43-45	
QS14	6:46-49	
QS19	9:57-62	"Foxes have holes; bury the dead"
QS20	10:1-11	Sending the 70 disciples
QS26	11:1-4	Lord's prayer
QS27	11:9-13	"Seek and ye shall find"
QS35	12:2-3	Speaking publicly

QS36	12:4-7	Fearing retaliation
QS38	12:13-21	Inheritance; parable of the rich fool
QS39	12:22-31	Worrying about the future
QS40	12:33-34	Give your possessions away
QS46	13:18-21	Mustard seed, leaven
QS50	14:11 & 18:14	Humility
QS51	14:16-24	The great supper
QS52	14:26-27 and 17:33	Anti-family sayings; saving life
QS53	14:34-35	Savorless salt

"Q2" - Describing Jesus as an Apocalyptic Prophet:

After the material of Q1 had been established as the doctrine of the newly formed Christian community other materials were added. Prophetic and apocalyptic elements were creeping in. Teaching was turning from a social gospel to a more apocalyptic vision. The new sayings were written in response to the serious civil unrest and upheavals in Palestine associated with the Roman-Jewish war. Another motivation was the rejection that they had experienced by their families and by the Jewish people generally. The new sayings were written circa 60 to 70 AD. These introduce us to John the Baptist and his disciples. The additions were meant to be passed off as the words of Jesus and John, even though the sayings were conceived by others three to four decades after Jesus' death. The sayings introduced in this period could be considered pseudepigrapha, which are writings using a famous person's name, in this case Jesus and John, to add validity to the words of an unknown author.

"Q3" - Retreat from the World

Additional sayings appear to have been added during the mid 70's AD. This was at a time that the Jews were driven from Palestine and The Roman-Jewish war had concluded. This places Q3 in the timeframe just after the book of Mark was written. This is why Mark did not contain Q3. As before, the sayings were falsely attributed to Jesus. Matthew and Luke would write their gospels using this version of Q, taking in all segments of Q1-Q3 and also incorporating the Gospel of Mark into their writings. The author of the Gospel of Thomas seems to have used the same material as that of Q1 and Q2 in his writing, but not the Q3 additions. Thomas was likely written before the evolution of the Q3 phase.

The common material in Q and Mark (cf. Mark 1.2; 1.7-8; 1.12-13; 3.22-26, 27-29; 4.21, 22, 24, 25; 4.30-32; 6.7-13; 8.11, 12; 8.34-35; 8.38; 9.37, 40, 42, 50; 10.10-11; 10.31; 11.22-23; 12.37b-40; 13.9, 11, 33-37) has repeatedly led to the hypothesis of a literary dependence of Mark on Q. But if Mark had known Q, his criteria for selecting the material he used, and especially the sayings he omitted, cannot be explained. The reasons given remain hypothetical. There are arguments for Mark as a supplement to the sayings source, and Q as supplement to Mark. Since Mark excludes parts of the Q material, one possibility is that Mark had access to the pre-redacted Q, and what we see included in Mark is the purer and earlier form of Q.

Helmut Koester states (op. cit., p. 150):
"The original version of Q must have included wisdom sayings as well as eschatological sayings. It cannot be argued that Q originally presented Jesus as a teacher of wisdom without an eschatological message. The close relationship of the *Gospel of Thomas* to Q cannot be accidental. Since the typical Son of Man sayings and announcements of judgments which are characteristic of the redaction of Q are never paralleled in the *Gospel of Thomas*, it is evident that its author had no knowledge of the final version of Q, nor of the secondary apocalyptic interpretation that the redactor of Q superimposed upon earlier eschatological sayings. The *Gospel of Thomas* is either dependent upon Q's earlier version or upon clusters of sayings employed in its composition.

For the followers of Jesus whose tradition is represented in the original composition of Q, the turning point of the ages is the proclamation of Jesus. He proclaims his teachings and announces the Kingdom is near. Judgment is coming. These sayings not only define the moment, they are also the rule of life for the community of the new age insofar as Jesus continues to speak in sayings of wisdom and in rules for the community. Jesus was viewed as the embodiment of heavenly Wisdom but his departure does not constitute a change in the urgency of the message. It increases it. Jesus' death would not be seen as a crisis of his proclamation. The disciples have as their task to carry on his proclamation. Any emphasis upon Jesus' suffering, death, and resurrection would be meaningless in this context, except to point out how evil the world had become, which to the Jews was quite obvious. "

Thus Q cannot be seen as a teaching supplement to Pauline theology at all. Q's theology and soteriology are fundamentally different from the doctrines Paul would later teach.

Helmut Koester states (op. cit., p. 165): "On the other hand, the Synoptic Sayings Source is an important piece of evidence for the continuation of a theology of followers of Jesus that had no relationship to the kerygma (message/preaching) of the cross and resurrection. It is evident now that this was not an isolated phenomenon. The opponents of Paul in 1 Corinthians 1-4, the *Gospel of Thomas*, the *Dialogue of the Savior*, and the opponents of the Gospel of John in the Johannine community all shared this understanding of the significance of Jesus' coming."

What does all this mean? In the beginning of the ministry of Jesus a small group of people took notes. They wrote down his sayings and deeds. One of these compilations became the Gospel of Thomas. The other became known as Q. This document, called Q, would go on to be used as one of sources of information for Matthew and Luke, but not before it had undergone many changes. Mark was also used as a foundation for Matthew and Luke. Mark may have had access to a version of Q, but if so it would have been an earlier version, before the additions and redactions. Knowing that Q was used as a gospel to the gospels, it seems fitting that we look at what was written before Matthew and Luke wrote their stories.

Following will be two versions of Q. The first is from a 1910 article, which uses Matthew and Luke to deduce the contents of Q. The second version is a more modern take on Q using the Gospel of Luke.

The Reconstructed Text of Q from the Sacred Texts Journals Christian Articles of THE OPEN COURT,

A MONTHLY MAGAZINE

Volume XXIV

CHICAGO, published by THE OPEN COURT PUBLISHING COMPANY 1910

THE GOSPEL SOURCE Q.

[Professor Wellhausen has discovered that both Matthew and Luke have used in addition to the Gospel of Mark another source (Quelle) which he designates by the initial Q, a name which has been generally adopted by theologians. The reconstruction here presented is according to Harnack.

The numbers which appear at the beginning of each fragment are the designations by which they are now referred to in theological literature. They follow upon the whole the order of Luke.

1.1

(Matt. iii. 5, 7-12; Luke iii. 3, 7-9, 16-17.)

(When from all the region around Jordan, John saw many [or: the multitudes] coming to baptism, he said unto them): O generation of vipers, who hath warned you to flee from the wrath to come? Bring forth therefore fruits meet for repentance; and think not [begin not] to say within yourselves: We have Abraham to our father, for I say unto you that God is able of these stones to raise up children unto Abraham. And now the axe is laid unto the root of the trees; therefore every tree which bringeth not forth good fruit is hewn down and cast into the fire. I baptize you with water unto repentance; but he that cometh after me is mightier than I, whose shoes I am not worthy to bear; he shall baptize you with (the [Holy] Ghost and) with fire; whose fan is in his hand, and he will thoroughly purge his floor, and gather his wheat unto the garner, but he will burn up the chaff with unquenchable fire.

(The baptism of Jesus, together with the descent of the Spirit and the voice from heaven.)

2.

(Matt. iv. 1-11; Luke iv. 1-13.)

Jesus was led up of the Spirit into the wilderness to be tempted of the devil, and when he had fasted forty days and forty nigh he was afterward an hungered, and the tempter said to him: If thou be the Son of God, command that these stones become bread, and he answered: It is written, Man shall not live by bread alone. Then he taketh him up to Jerusalem and setteth him on the pinnacle of the temple, and saith to him: If thou be the Son of God, cast thyself down; for it is written, He shall give his angels charge concerning thee, and in their hands they shall bear thee up lest at any time thou dash thy foot against a stone. Jesus said to him: Again it is written, Thou shalt not tempt the Lord thy God. Again he taketh him up unto an exceeding high mountain and sheweth him all the kingdoms of the world and the glory of them; and said unto him: All these things will I give thee, if thou wilt worship me. And Jesus saith unto him: It is written, The Lord thy God shalt thou worship and him only shalt thou serve. And the devil leaveth him.

3.

(Matt. v. 1-4, 6, 11, 12; Luke vi. 17, 20-23.)

(... multitudes ... he taught his disciples, saying ...)

Blessed are the poor in spirit, for theirs is the kingdom of God;

Blessed are they that mourn, for they shall be comforted;

Blessed are they that hunger, for they shall be filled;

Blessed are ye, when men shall revile you and persecute you and shall say all manner of evil against you falsely. Rejoice and be exceeding glad, for great is your reward in heaven; for so persecuted they the prophets which were before you.

4.

(Matt. v. 39-40; Luke vi. 29.)

Whosoever shall smite thee on the (thy right) cheek turn to him the other also; and if any man will sue thee at the law and take away thy coat, let him have thy cloak also.

5.

(Matt. v. 42; Luke vi. 30.)

Give to him that asketh thee, and from him that would borrow of thee turn not thou away.

6.

(Matt. v. 44-48; Luke vi. 27, 28, 35b, 32, 33, 36.)

I say unto you: Love your enemies and pray for them which persecute you, that ye may be the sons of your Father, for he maketh the sun to rise on the evil and on the good (and sendeth rain on the just and on the unjust). For if ye love them which love you, what reward have ye? Do not even the publicans the same? And if ye salute your brethren only, what do ye more than others? Do not even the Gentiles the same? Be ye therefore merciful as your Father is merciful.

7.

(Matt. vii. 12; Luke vi. 31.)

All things whatsoever ye would that men should do to you, do ye even so to them.

8.

(Matt. vii. 1-5; Luke vi. 37, 38, 41, 42.)

Judge not, that ye be not judged; for with what judgment ye judge, ye shall be judged; and with what measure ye mete, it shall be measured to you again. And why beholdest thou the mote that is in thy brother's eye, but considerest not the beam that is in thine own eye? Or how wilt thou say to thy brother: Let me cast out the mote out of thine eye; and behold, a beam is in thine own eye? Thou hypocrite, first cast out the beam out of thine own eye, and then shalt thou see clearly to cast out the mote out of thy brother's eye.

11.

(Matt. vii. 16-18; xii. 33; Luke vi. 43-44.)

The tree is known by the fruit. Do men gather grapes of thorns, or figs of thistles? Even so every good tree bringeth forth good fruit, but a corrupt tree bringeth forth evil fruit. A good tree cannot bring forth evil fruit, neither can a corrupt tree bring forth good fruit.

12.

(Matt. vii. 21, 24-27; Luke vi. 46-49.)

(Not everyone that saith unto me: Lord, Lord! shall enter into the kingdom of God, but he that doeth the will of the Father.) Therefore whosoever heareth these sayings of mine and doeth them, I will shew you whom he is like. He is like (or in place of the last; twelve words: He shall be likened) unto a man which built his house upon a rock. And the rain descended, and the floods came, and the winds blew and beat upon that house, and it fell not; for it was founded upon a rock. And every one that heareth these sayings of mine and doeth them not, shall be likened unto a man which built his house upon the sand. And the rain descended and the floods came, and the winds blew and beat upon that house, and it fell, and great was the fall of it.

9.

(Matt. xv. 14; Luke vi. 39.)

If the blind lead the blind, both shall fall into the ditch.

27.

(Matt. vi. 9, 11-13; Luke xi. 2-4.)

(Father, give us this day our daily bread, and forgive us our debts, as we forgive our debtors, and lead us not into temptation.)

28.

(Matt. vii. 7-11; Luke xi. 9-13.)

Ask, and it shall be given you; seek, and ye shall find; knock, and it shall be opened unto you. For every one that asketh receiveth; and he that seeketh findeth; and to him that knocketh it shall be opened. Or what man is there of you, whom if his son ask bread, will he give him a stone? Or if he ask for fish, will he give him a serpent? If ye then, being evil, know how to give good things (gifts) to your children, how much more will the Father from heaven give good things to them that ask him.

31.

(Matt. v. 15; Luke xi. 33.)

Men do not light a candle and place it under a bushel, but on candlestick; and it giveth light unto all that are in the house.

32.

(Matt. vi. 22, 23; Luke xii. 34-35.)

The light of the body is the (thine) eye; if therefore thine eye be single (generous, unclouded), thy whole body shall be full of light; but if thine eye be evil (selfish, of poor sight), thy whole body shall be full of darkness. If therefore the light that is in thee be darkened, how great is that darkness [scil. in the whole]!

35.

(Matt. vi. 25-33; Luke xii. 22-31.)

Therefore I say unto you: Take no thought for your life, what ye shall eat; nor yet for your body, what ye shall put on. Is not the life more than meat and the body more than raiment? Behold the ravens (or: the fowls of the air); for they sow not, neither do they reap nor gather into barns; yet God feedeth them. Are ye not much better than they? Which of you by taking thought can add one cubit unto his stature? and why take ye thought for raiment? Consider the lilies, how they grow? They toil not, neither do they spin; and yet I say unto you (that) even Solomon în all his glory was not arrayed like one of these. Wherefore if God so clothe the grass of the field which to-day is, and to-morrow is cast into the oven shall he not much more clothe you, O ye of little faith? Therefore take no thought saying: What shall we eat? or What shall we drink? or Wherewithall shall we be clothed? For after all these things do the nations (of the world) seek; for your Father knoweth that ye have need of all these things. But seek ye his kingdom, and all these things shall be added unto you.

36.

(Matt. vi. 19-21; Luke xii. 33-34.)

Lay not up for yourselves treasures upon earth, where moth and rust doth corrupt, and where thieves break through and steal: but lay up for yourselves treasures in heaven, where neither moth nor rust doth corrupt, and where theives do not break through nor steal; for where thy (your) treasure is, there will thy (your) heart be also.

39.

(Matt. v. 25-26; Luke xii. 58-59.)

Agree with thine adversary quickly, whiles thou art in the way with him; lest at any time the adversary deliver thee to the judge and the judge to the officer and thou be cast into prison. (Verily) I

Before the Gospels

say unto thee, thou shalt by no means come out thence, till thou hast paid the uttermost farthing.

41.

(Matt. vii. 13-14; Luke xiii. 24.)

Enter ye in at the strait gate; for wide (is the gate) and broad is the way that leadeth to destruction, and many there be which go in thereat. Because strait is the gate and narrow is the way which leadeth unto life, and few there be that find it.

47.

(Matt. v. 13; Luke xiv. 34-35.)

Ye are the salt (of the earth); but if the salt have lost its savour, wherewith shall it be salted? It is thenceforth good for nothing but to be cast out and to be trodden under foot of men.

49.

(Matt. vi. 24; Luke xvi. 13.)

No man can serve two masters; for either he will hate the one and love the other, or else he will hold to the one and despise the other. Ye cannot serve God and mammon.

51.

(Matt. v. 18; Luke xvi. 17.)

(Verily I say unto you): Till heaven and earth pass, one jot or one tittle shall in no wise pass from the law.

52.

(Matt. v. 32; Luke xvi. 18.)

(I say unto you: Whosoever shall put away his wife causeth her to commit adultery, and whosoever shall marry her that is divorced committeth adultery.

13.

(Matt. vii. 28; viii. 5-10, 13; Luke vii. 1-10.)

He entered into Capernaum, and there came unto him a centurion beseeching him and saying: Lord, my servant lieth at home sick of the palsy, grievously tormented. He saith unto him: I will come and heal him. The centurion answered and said: Lord, I am not worthy that thou shouldest come under my roof; but speak the word only and my servant shall be healed. For I am a man under authority, having soldiers under me, and I say to this man, Go, and he goeth; and to another, Come, and he cometh; and to my slave: Do this, and he doeth it. When Jesus heard it he marvelled and said to them that followed, (Verily) I say unto you, Not even in Israel have I found such faith. (And Jesus said to the centurion: [Go thy way;] as thou hast believed, be it done unto thee. And the servant was healed in the selfsame hour.)

17.

(Matt. viii. 19-22; Luke ix. 57-60.)

(Someone said to him): I will follow thee whithersoever thou goest; and Jesus saith unto him: The foxes have holes, and the birds of the air have nests; but the Son of man hath not where to lay his head. Another said to him: Suffer me first to go and bury my father; but he saith unto him: Follow me, and let the dead bury their dead.

18.

(Matt. ix. 37-38; Luke x. 2.)

He saith unto them (or: to his disciples): The harvest truly is plenteous, but the labourers are few; pray ye therefore the Lord of the harvest that he will send forth labourers into his harvest.

16.

(Matt. x. 7; Luke ix. 2; x. 9-11.)

As ye go, preach, saying that the kingdom of God is at hand.

20.

(Matt. x. 12-13; Luke x. 4-6.)

(Carry neither purse, nor scrip, nor shoes, and salute no man by the way) And when ye come into a house, salute it; and if the house be worthy, let your peace come upon it; but if it be not worthy, let your peace return to you.

21.

(Matt. x. 10b; Luke x. 7.)

(And in the same house remain, eating and drinking such things as they give); for the labourer is worthy of his hire.

22.

(Matt. x. 15; Luke x. 8-12.)

(. . . Into whatsoever city ye enter and they receive you, eat such things as are set before you and say unto them: The kingdom of God is at hand. But into whatsoever city ye enter and they receive you not, go your ways out into the streets of the same and say: Even the very dust of your city which cleaveth to our feet do we wipe off against you). (Verily) I say unto you: It shall be more tolerable for the land of Sodom and Gomorrha (or in place of the last six words: Sodom) in that day (or: in the day of judgment) than for that city.

19:

(Matt. v. 16a; Luke x. 3.)

Behold I send you forth as sheep in the midst of wolves.

34a.

(Matt. x. 26-33; Luke xii. 2-9.)

There is nothing covered that shall not be revealed, and hid that shall not be known. What I tell you in darkness that speak ye in light; and what ye hear in the ear that preach ye upon the housetops. And fear not them which kill the body but are not able to kill the soul; but rather fear him which is able to destroy both soul and body in hell. Are not two (five) sparrows sold for a farthing (two farthings)? And one of them shall not fall on the ground without God. But the very hairs of your head are all numbered. Fear ye not (therefore), ye are of (much) more value than (many) sparrows. Whosoever therefore shall confess me before men, him will the Son of man (or: I) confess also before the angels of God; but whosoever shall deny me before men, him will I also deny before the angels of God.

34b.

(Matt. xii. 32; Luke xii. 10.)

... And whosoever speaketh a word against the Son of man, it shall be forgiven him; but whosoever speaketh (a word) against the Holy Ghost, it shall not be forgiven him.

38.

(Matt. x. 34-36; Luke xii. 51, 53.)

Think ye that I came to send peace on earth? I came not to send peace, but a sword. For I came to set a man at variance against his father, and the daughter against her mother, and the daughter-in-law against her mother-in-law. (And a man's foes shall be they of his own household.)

45.

(Matt. x. 37; Luke xiv. 26.)

(He that loveth father and mother more than me, is not worthy of me; and he that loveth son or daughter more than me, is not worthy of me.)

46.

(Matt. x. 38; Luke xiv. 27.)

He that taketh not his cross and followeth after me is not worthy of me.

57.

(Matt. x. 39; Luke xvii. 33.)

He that findeth his soul shall lose it, and he that loseth his soul shall find it.

10.

(Matt. x. 24-25; Luke vi. 40.)

The disciple is not above his master, nor the servant above his lord. It is enough for the disciple that he be as his master, and the servant as his lord.

24.

(Matt. x. 40; Luke x. 16)

(He that receiveth you receiveth me, and he that receiveth me receiveth him that sent me.)

14.

(Matt. xi. 2-11; Luke vii. 18-28.)

Now when John had heard in the prison the works of Christ, he sent his disciples and said unto him: Art thou he that should come, or do we look for another? And he answered and said unto them: Go and shew John again those things which ye do hear and see, the blind receive their sight, and the lame walk, the lepers are cleansed, and the deaf hear, the dead are raised up, and the poor have the gospel preached to them; and blessed is he whosoever shall not be offended in me. And as they departed, he began to say unto the multitudes concerning John: What went ye out into the wilderness to see? A reed shaken with the wind? But what went ye out for to see? A man clothed in soft raiment? Behold they that wear soft clothing are in kings' houses! But what went ye out for to see? A prophet? Yea, I say unto you, and more than a prophet! For this is he of whom it is written: Behold I send my messenger before thy face, which shall prepare thy way before thee. (Verily) I say unto you among them that are born of women there hath not risen a greater than John (the Baptist); notwithstanding he that is least in the kingdom of God is greater than he. . . .

50.

(Matt. xi. 12-13; Luke xvi. 16.)

The prophets and the law were until John; since that time the kingdom of God suffereth violence, and the violent take it by force (or: From the days of John until now the kingdom of God, etc.: for all the prophets and the law prophesied until John) . . .

15.

(Matt. xi. 16-10; Luke vii. 31-35;)

Whereunto shall I liken this generation (and to what is it like)? It is like unto children sitting in the markets and calling unto their fellows, saying: We have piped unto you, and ye have not danced; we have mourned unto you, and ye have not lamented. For John came neither eating nor drinking, and they say: He hath a devil! The Son of man came eating and drinking, and they say, Behold a man gluttonous and a winebibber, a friend of publicans and sinners! But wisdom is justified of her children.

23.

(Matt. xi. 21-23; Luke x. 13-15.)

Woe unto thee, Chorazin! woe unto thee, Bethsaida! For if the mighty works which were done in you had been done in Tyre and Sidon, they would have repented long ago in sackcloth and ashes. But (I say unto you) it shall be more tolerable for Tyre and Sidon (at the day of judgment, or: at the judgment) than for you. And thou

Capernaum shalt thou have been exalted to heaven? To hell shalt thou be cast down.

25.

(Matt. xi. 25-27; Luke x. 21-22.)

At that time he said: I thank thee, O Father, Lord of heaven and earth, because thou hast hid these things from the wise and prudent, and hast revealed them unto babes; even so [I thank thee] Father, for so it seemed good in thy sight. All things are delivered unto me of my Father, and no man knoweth (the Son but the Father, neither knoweth any man) the Father save the Son, and he to whomsoever the Son will reveal him.

26.

(Matt. xiii. 16-17; Luke x. 23b-24.)

Blessed are your eyes, for they see, and (your) ears, for they hear; (for verily) I say unto you that many prophets (and kings) have desired to see those things which ye see and have not seen them, and to hear those things which ye hear and have not heard them.

29.

(Matt. xii. 22-23, 25, 27-28, 30, 43-45; Luke xi. 14, 17, 19, 20, 23-26.)

(He healed) a dumb man possessed with a devil, (insomuch that) the dumb spake and the multitudes (all) were amazed . . . every kingdom divided against itself is brought to desolation . . . and if I by Beelzebub cast out devils, by whom do yout children cast them out? therefore they shall be your judges. But if I cast out devils by the Spirit of God, then the kingdom of God is come unto you . . . He that is not with me is against me, and he that gathereth not with me scattereth abroad . . . When the unclean spirit is gone out of a man he walketh through dry places seeking rest and findeth none. (Then) he saith, I will return into my house from whence I came out; and when he is come he findeth it empty (and) swept and garnished. Then goeth he and taketh with himself seven other spirits more wicked than himself, and they enter in and dwell there, and the last state of that man is worse than the first.

30.

(Matt. xii. 38-39, 41-42; Luke xi. 16, 29-32.)

We would see a sign from thee. But he said: An evil and adulterous generation seeketh after a sign, and there shall no sign be given to it but the sign of Jonah. For as Jonah was a sign unto the Ninevites, so shall also the Son of man be to this generation. The men of Nineveh shall rise in judgment with this generation, and shall condemn it, because they repented at the preaching of Jonah, and behold a greater than Jonah is here. The queen of the south shall rise up in the judgment with this generation and shall condemn it, for she came from the uttermost parts of the earth to hear the wisdom of Solomon, and behold a greater than Solomon is here.

40.

(Matt. xiii. 31-33; Luke xiii. 18-21.)

(Unto what is the kingdom of God like? and to what shall I liken it? It is like to a grain of mustard seed which a man took and sowed in his field, and it grew and becameth a tree, and the birds of the air lodged in the branches thereof.)

(And again he said): To what shall I liken the kingdom of God? It is like unto leaven which a woman took and hid in three measures of meal till the whole was leavened.

44.

(Matt. xxiii. 12; Luke xiv. 11.)

Whosoever exalteth himself shall be abased, and he that humbleth himself shall be exalted.

42.

(Matt. viii. 11-12; Luke xiii. 28-29.)

I say unto you: They shall come from the east and from the west, and shall sit down with Abraham and Isaac and Jacob in the kingdom of God; but the children of the kingdom shall be cast out; there shall be weeping and gnashing of teeth.

48.

(Matt. xviii. 12-13; Luke xv. 4-7.)

How think ye? If a man have an hundred sheep, and one of them be gone astray, doth he not leave the ninety and nine upon the mountains, and go and seek that which has gone astray? And if so be that he find it, (verily) I say unto you he rejoiceth more of it than of the ninety and nine which went not astray.

53.

(Matt. xviii. 7; Luke xvii. 1.)

It must needs be that offenses come; but woe to that man by the offense cometh.

54.

(Matt. xviii. 15, 21-22; Luke xvii. 3-4.)

If thy brother shall trespass against thee, tell him his fault; if he shall hear thee, thou hast gained thy brother . . . How oft shall my brother sin against me and I forgive him? till seven times? Jesus saith unto him: I say not unto thee, Until seven times; but, Until seventy times seven.

55.

(Matt. xvii. 20b; Luke xvii. 6.)

If ye have faith as a grain of mustard seed, ye shall say unto this mountain: Remove from hence to yonder place, and it shall remove.

33.

(Matt. xxiii. 4, 13, 23, 25, 27, 29, 30-32, 34-36; Luke xi. 46, 52, 42, 39, 44, 47-52.)

. . . They bind heavy burdens and lay them on men's shoulders, and they themselves will not move them with one of their fingers.

Woe unto you, Pharisees! for ye shut up the kingdom of God against men; for ye neither go in yourselves, neither suffer ye them that are entering to go in.

Woe unto you, Pharisees! for ye pay tithe of mint and anise and cummin, and have omitted the weightier matters of the law, judgment and mercy.

Now ye Pharisees! ye make clean the outside of the cup and of the platter, but within they are full; of extortion and excess.

(Luke xi. 44.) Woe unto you, for ye are as sepulchers which appear not, and the men that walk over them are not aware of them.

(Matt. xxiii. 27.) (Woe unto you, Pharisees! for ye are like unto whited (white washed) sepulchers, which indeed appear beautiful outward, but within are full of dead men's bones and of all uncleanness.)

Woe unto you! because ye build the tombs of the prophets and say: If we had been in the days of our fathers we would not have been partakers with them in the blood of the prophets. Wherefore ye be witnesses against yourselves that ye are the children of them which killed the prophets, (and now fulfill the measure of your fathers)!

Wherefore also the Wisdom of God said: I send unto you prophets and wise men and scribes; some of them ye shall kill and persecute; that upon you may come all the blood shed upon the earth from the blood of Abel unto the blood of Zacharias, whom ye slew between the temple and the altar. Verily I say unto you, All these things shall come upon this generation.

43.

(Matt. xxiii. 37-39; Luke xiii. 34-35.)

O Jerusalem! Jerusalem! thou that killest the prophets and stonest them which are sent unto thee! How often would I have gathered thy children together, even as a hen (gathereth) her chicks under her wings, and ye would not! Behold your house is left unto you desolate. (For) I say unto you: Ye shall not see me henceforth till (it shall come when) ye shall say: Blessed is he that cometh in the name of the Lord.

56.

(Matt. xxiv. 26-28, 37-41; Luke xvii. 23-24, 37, 26-27, 34-35.)

Wherefore if they shall say unto you: Behold, he is in the desert! Go ye not forth. Behold, he is in the secret chambers! Believe it not. For as the lightning cometh out of the east and shineth even unto the west, so shall also the coming of the Son of man be. For wheresoever the carcase is, there will the eagles be gathered together.

As the days of Noah were, so shall also the coming of the Son of man be. For as in the days that were before the flood they were eating and drinking, marrying and giving in marriage, until the day that Noah entered into the ark, and knew not until the flood came and took them all away, so shall also the coming of the Son of man be. There shall be two in the field, one shall be taken and the other left; two women shall be grinding at the mill, the one shall be taken and the other left.

37.

(Matt. xxiv. 43-51; Luke xii. 39-40, 42-46.)

But know this, that if the goodman of the house had known in what watch the thief would come, he would have watched and would not have suffered his house to be broken up. (Therefore be ye also ready, for in such an hour as ye think not the Son of man cometh.) Who then is a faithful and wise servant whom his lord hath made ruler over his household to give them meat in due season? Blessed is that servant whom his lord when he cometh shall find so doing. Verily I say unto you, that he shall make him rule over all his goods. But and if that (evil) servant shall say in his heart: My lord delayeth his coming, and shall begin to smite his fellow servants, and to eat and drink with the drunken, the lord of that servant shall come in a day when he looketh not for him, and in an hour that he is not aware of, and shall cut him asunder and appoint him his portion with the hypocrites.

58.

(Matt. xxv. 29; Luke xix. 26.)

Unto him (everyone) that hath shall be given, and he shall have abundance; but from him that hath not, shall be taken away even that which he hath.

59.

(Matt. xix. 28; Luke xxii. 28, 30.)

Ye who have followed me . . . shall sit upon twelve thrones. judging the twelve tribes of Israel.

Here is a more modern look at Q using New Revised Standard version of the Bible. More modern and in depth research has yielded a slightly different extraction of Q. The Book of Luke is used as the extraction point:

LUKE 3:7-9 John said to the crowds that came out to be baptized by him, "You brood of vipers! Who warned you to flee from the wrath to come? 8 Bear fruits worthy of repentance. Do not begin to say to yourselves, `We have Abraham as our ancestor'; for I tell you, God is able from these stones to raise up children to Abraham. 9 Even now the ax is lying at the root of the trees; every tree therefore that does not bear good fruit is cut down and thrown into the fire."

3:16-17 John answered all of them by saying, "I baptize you with water; but one who is more powerful than I is coming; I am not worthy to untie the thong of his sandals. He will baptize you with the Holy Spirit and fire. 17 His winnowing fork is in his hand, to clear his threshing floor and to gather the wheat into his granary; but the chaff he will burn with unquenchable fire."

4:1-13 Jesus, full of the Holy Spirit, returned from the Jordan and was led by the Spirit in the wilderness, 2 where for forty days he was tempted by the devil. He ate nothing at all during those days, and when they were over, he was famished. 3 The devil said to him, "If you are the Son of God, command this stone to become a loaf of bread." 4 Jesus answered him, "It is written, `One does not live by bread alone.'" 5 Then the devil led him up and showed him in an instant all the kingdoms of the world. 6 And the devil said to him, "To you I will give their glory and all this authority; for it has been given over to me, and I give it to anyone I please. 7 If you, then, will worship me, it will all be yours." 8 Jesus answered him, "It is written, `Worship the Lord your God, and serve only him.'" 9 Then the devil took him to Jerusalem, and placed him on the pinnacle of the temple, saying to him, "If you are the Son of God, throw yourself down from here, 10 for it is written, `He will command his angels concerning you, to protect you,' 11 and `On their hands they will bear you up, so that you will not dash your foot against a stone.'" 12 Jesus answered him, "It is said, `Do not put the Lord your God to the test.'" 13 When the devil had finished every test, he departed from him until an opportune time.

6:12, 17, 20 Now during those days he went out to the mountain to pray; and he spent the night in prayer to God. 17 He came down with them and stood on a level place, with a great crowd of his disciples and a great multitude of people from all Judea, Jerusalem, and the coast of Tyre and Sidon. 20 Then he looked up at his disciples and said:

6:20-26 "Blessed are you who are poor, for yours is the kingdom of God. 21 "Blessed are you who are hungry now, for you will be filled. "Blessed are you who weep now, for you will laugh. 22 "Blessed are you when people hate you, and when they exclude you, revile you, and defame you on account of the Son of Man. 23

Rejoice in that day and leap for joy, for surely your reward is great in heaven; for that is what their ancestors did to the prophets. 24 "But woe to you who are rich, for you have received your consolation. 25 "Woe to you who are full now, for you will be hungry. "Woe to you who are laughing now, for you will mourn and weep. 26 "Woe to you when all speak well of you, for that is what their ancestors did to the false prophets.

6:27-36 "But I say to you that listen, Love your enemies, do good to those who hate you, 28 bless those who curse you, pray for those who abuse you. 29 If anyone strikes you on the cheek, offer the other also; and from anyone who takes away your coat do not withhold even your shirt. 30 Give to everyone who begs from you; and if anyone takes away your goods, do not ask for them again. 31 Do to others as you would have them do to you. 32 "If you love those who love you, what credit is that to you? For even sinners love those who love them. 33 If you do good to those who do good to you, what credit is that to you? For even sinners do the same. 34 If you lend to those from whom you hope to receive, what credit is that to you? Even sinners lend to sinners, to receive as much again. 35 But love your enemies, do good, and lend, expecting nothing in return. Your reward will be great, and you will be children of the Most High; for he is kind to the ungrateful and the wicked. 36 Be merciful, just as your Father is merciful.

6:37-38 "Do not judge, and you will not be judged; do not condemn, and you will not be condemned. Forgive, and you will be forgiven;

38 give, and it will be given to you. A good measure, pressed down, shaken together, running over, will be put into your lap; for the measure you give will be the measure you get back."

6:39-40 He also told them a parable: "Can a blind person guide a blind person? Will not both fall into a pit? 40 A disciple is not above the teacher, but everyone who is fully qualified will be like the teacher.

6:41-42 Why do you see the speck in your neighbor's eye, but do not notice the log in your own eye? 42 Or how can you say to your neighbor, `Friend, let me take out the speck in your eye,' when you yourself do not see the log in your own eye? You hypocrite, first take the log out of your own eye, and then you will see clearly to take the speck out of your neighbor's eye.

6:43-45 "No good tree bears bad fruit, nor again does a bad tree bear good fruit; 44 for each tree is known by its own fruit. Figs are not gathered from thorns, nor are grapes picked from a bramble bush. 45 The good person out of the good treasure of the heart produces good, and the evil person out of evil treasure produces evil; for it is out of the abundance of the heart that the mouth speaks.

6:46-49 "Why do you call me `Lord, Lord,' and do not do what I tell you? 47 I will show you what someone is like who comes to me, hears my words, and acts on them. 48 That one is like a man building a house, who dug deeply and laid the foundation on rock;

when a flood arose, the river burst against that house but could not shake it, because it had been well built. 49 But the one who hears and does not act is like a man who built a house on the ground without a foundation. When the river burst against it, immediately it fell, and great was the ruin of that house."

7:1-10 After Jesus had finished all his sayings in the hearing of the people, he entered Capernaum. 2 A centurion there had a slave whom he valued highly, and who was ill and close to death. 3 When he heard about Jesus, he sent some Jewish elders to him, asking him to come and heal his slave. 4 When they came to Jesus, they appealed to him earnestly, saying, "He is worthy of having you do this for him, 5 for he loves our people, and it is he who built our synagogue for us." 6 And Jesus went with them, but when he was not far from the house, the centurion sent friends to say to him, "Lord, do not trouble yourself, for I am not worthy to have you come under my roof; 7 therefore I did not presume to come to you. But only speak the word, and let my servant be healed. 8 For I also am a man set under authority, with soldiers under me; and I say to one, `Go,' and he goes, and to another, `Come,' and he comes, and to my slave, `Do this,' and the slave does it." 9 When Jesus heard this he was amazed at him, and turning to the crowd that followed him, he said, "I tell you, not even in Israel have I found such faith." 10 When those who had been sent returned to the house, they found the slave in good health.

7:18-20, 22-23 The disciples of John reported all these things to him. So John summoned two of his disciples 19 and sent them to the Lord to ask, "Are you the one who is to come, or are we to wait for another?" 20 When the men had come to him, they said, "John the Baptist has sent us to you to ask, `Are you the one who is to come, or are we to wait for another?'" 22 And he answered them, "Go and tell John what you have seen and heard: the blind receive their sight, the lame walk, the lepers are cleansed, the deaf hear, the dead are raised, the poor have good news brought to them. 23 And blessed is anyone who takes no offense at me."

7:24-28 When John's messengers had gone, Jesus began to speak to the crowds about John: "What did you go out into the wilderness to look at? A reed shaken by the wind? 25 What then did you go out to see? Someone dressed in soft robes? Look, those who put on fine clothing and live in luxury are in royal palaces. 26 What then did you go out to see? A prophet? Yes, I tell you, and more than a prophet. 27 This is the one about whom it is written, `See, I am sending my messenger ahead of you, who will prepare your way before you.' 28 I tell you, among those born of women no one is greater than John; yet the least in the kingdom of God is greater than he."

7:31-35 "To what then will I compare the people of this generation, and what are they like? 32 They are like children sitting in the marketplace and calling to one another, `We played the flute for you, and you did not dance; we wailed, and you did not weep.' 33 For John the Baptist has come eating no bread and drinking no wine, and you say, `He has a demon'; 34 the Son of Man has come eating and drinking, and you say, `Look, a glutton and a drunkard, a friend of tax collectors and sinners!' 35 Nevertheless, wisdom is vindicated by all her children."

9:57-62 As they were going along the road, someone said to him, "I will follow you wherever you go." 58 And Jesus said to him, "Foxes have holes, and birds of the air have nests; but the Son of Man has nowhere to lay his head." 59 To another he said, "Follow me." But he said, "Lord, first let me go and bury my father." 60 But Jesus said to him, "Let the dead bury their own dead; but as for you, go and proclaim the kingdom of God." 61 Another said, "I will follow you, Lord; but let me first say farewell to those at my home." 62 Jesus said to him, "No one who puts a hand to the plow and looks back is fit for the kingdom of God."

10:2-12 He said to them, "The harvest is plentiful, but the laborers are few; therefore ask the Lord of the harvest to send out laborers into his harvest. 3 Go on your way. See, I am sending you out like lambs into the midst of wolves. 4 Carry no purse, no bag, no sandals; and greet no one on the road. 5 Whatever house you enter, first say, `Peace to this house!' 6 And if anyone is there who shares in peace, your peace will rest on that person; but if not, it will return to you. 7 Remain in the same house, eating and drinking whatever they provide, for the laborer deserves to be paid. Do not move about from house to house. 8 Whenever you enter a town and its people welcome you, eat what is set before you; 9 cure the sick who are there, and say to them, `The kingdom of God has come near to you.'  10 But whenever you enter a town and they do not welcome you, go out into its streets and say,  11 `Even the dust of your town that clings to our feet, we wipe off in protest against you. Yet know this: the kingdom of God has come near.' 12 I tell you, on that day it will be more tolerable for Sodom than for that town.

10:13-15 "Woe to you, Chorazin! Woe to you, Bethsaida! For if the deeds of power done in you had been done in Tyre and Sidon, they would have repented long ago, sitting in sackcloth and ashes. 14 But at the judgment it will be more tolerable for Tyre and Sidon than for you. 15 And you, Capernaum, will you be exalted to heaven? No, you will be brought down to Hades.

10:16 "Whoever listens to you listens to me, and whoever rejects you rejects me, and whoever rejects me rejects the one who sent me."

10:21-22 At that same hour Jesus rejoiced in the Holy Spirit and said, "I thank you, Father, Lord of heaven and earth, because you have hidden these things from the wise and the intelligent and have revealed them to infants; yes, Father, for such was your gracious will. 22 All things have been handed over to me by my Father; and no one knows who the Son is except the Father, or who the Father is except the Son and anyone to whom the Son chooses to reveal him."

10:23-24 Then turning to the disciples, Jesus said to them privately, "Blessed are the eyes that see what you see! 24 For I tell you that many prophets and kings desired to see what you see, but did not see it, and to hear what you hear, but did not hear it."

11:2-4 He said to them, "When you pray, say: Father, hallowed be your name. Your kingdom come. 3 Give us each day our daily bread. 4 And forgive us our sins, for we ourselves forgive everyone indebted to us. And do not bring us to the time of trial."

11:9-13 "So I say to you, Ask, and it will be given you; search, and you will find; knock, and the door will be opened for you. 10 For everyone who asks receives, and everyone who searches finds, and for everyone who knocks, the door will be opened. 11 Is there anyone among you who, if your child asks for a fish, will give a snake instead of a fish? 12 Or if the child asks for an egg, will give a scorpion? 13 If you then, who are evil, know how to give good gifts to your children, how much more will the heavenly Father give the Holy Spirit to those who ask him!"

11:14-23 Now he was casting out a demon that was mute; when the demon had gone out, the one who had been mute spoke, and the crowds were amazed. 15 But some of them said, "He casts out demons by Beelzebul, the ruler of the demons." 17 But he knew what they were thinking and said to them, "Every kingdom divided against itself becomes a desert, and house falls on house. 18 If

Satan also is divided against himself, how will his kingdom stand? -- for you say that I cast out the demons by Beelzebul. 19 Now if I cast out the demons by Beelzebul, by whom do your exorcists cast them out? Therefore they will be your judges. 20 But if it is by the finger of God that I cast out the demons, then the kingdom of God has come to you. 21 When a strong man, fully armed, guards his castle, his property is safe. 22 But when one stronger than he attacks him and overpowers him, he takes away his armor in which he trusted and divides his plunder. 23 Whoever is not with me is against me, and whoever does not gather with me scatters.

11:24-26 "When the unclean spirit has gone out of a person, it wanders through waterless regions looking for a resting place, but not finding any, it says, `I will return to my house from which I came.' 25 When it comes, it finds it swept and put in order. 26 Then it goes and brings seven other spirits more evil than itself, and they enter and live there; and the last state of that person is worse than the first."

11:27-28 While he was saying this, a woman in the crowd raised her voice and said to him, "Blessed is the womb that bore you and the breasts that nursed you!" 28 But he said, "Blessed rather are those who hear the word of God and obey it!"

11:16, 29-32 16 Others, to test him, kept demanding from him a sign from heaven. 29 When the crowds were increasing, he began to say, "This generation is an evil generation; it asks for a sign, but no sign

Before the Gospels

will be given to it except the sign of Jonah. 30 For just as Jonah became a sign to the people of Nineveh, so the Son of Man will be to this generation. 31 The queen of the South will rise at the judgment with the people of this generation and condemn them, because she came from the ends of the earth to listen to the wisdom of Solomon, and see, something greater than Solomon is here! 32 The people of Nineveh will rise up at the judgment with this generation and condemn it, because they repented at the proclamation of Jonah, and see, something greater than Jonah is here!

11:33 "No one after lighting a lamp puts it in a cellar, but on the lampstand so that those who enter may see the light.

11:34-36 Your eye is the lamp of your body. If your eye is healthy, your whole body is full of light; but if it is not healthy, your body is full of darkness. 35 Therefore consider whether the light in you is not darkness. 36 If then your whole body is full of light, with no part of it in darkness, it will be as full of light as when a lamp gives you light with its rays."

11:42 "But woe to you Pharisees! For you tithe mint and rue and herbs of all kinds, and neglect justice and the love of God; it is these you ought to have practiced, without neglecting the others.

11:39-41 Then the Lord said to him, "Now you Pharisees clean the outside of the cup and of the dish, but inside you are full of greed and wickedness. 40 You fools! Did not the one who made the outside make the inside also? 41 So give for alms those things that are within; and see, everything will be clean for you.

11:43 Woe to you Pharisees! For you love to have the seat of honor in the synagogues and to be greeted with respect in the marketplaces.

11:44 Woe to you! For you are like unmarked graves, and people walk over them without realizing it."

11:46 And he said, "Woe also to you lawyers! For you load people with burdens hard to bear, and you yourselves do not lift a finger to ease them.

11:47-48 Woe to you! For you build the tombs of the prophets whom your ancestors killed. 48 So you are witnesses and approve of the deeds of your ancestors; for they killed them, and you build their tombs.

11:49-51 Therefore also the Wisdom of God said, `I will send them prophets and apostles, some of whom they will kill and persecute,' 50 so that this generation may be charged with the blood of all the prophets shed since the foundation of the world, 51 from the blood of Abel to the blood of Zechariah, who perished between the altar and the sanctuary. Yes, I tell you, it will be charged against this generation.

11:52 Woe to you lawyers! For you have taken away the key of knowledge; you did not enter yourselves, and you hindered those who were entering."

12:2-3 Nothing is covered up that will not be uncovered, and nothing secret that will not become known. 3 Therefore whatever you have said in the dark will be heard in the light, and what you have whispered behind closed doors will be proclaimed from the housetops.

12:4-7 "I tell you, my friends, do not fear those who kill the body, and after that can do nothing more. 5 But I will warn you whom to fear: fear him who, after he has killed, has authority to cast into hell. Yes, I tell you, fear him! 6 Are not five sparrows sold for two pennies? Yet not one of them is forgotten in God's sight. 7 But even the hairs of your head are all counted. Do not be afraid; you are of more value than many sparrows.

12:8-9 "And I tell you, everyone who acknowledges me before others, the Son of Man also will acknowledge before the angels of God; 9 but whoever denies me before others will be denied before the angels of God.

12:10 And everyone who speaks a word against the Son of Man will be forgiven; but whoever blasphemes against the Holy Spirit will not be forgiven.

12:11-12 When they bring you before the synagogues, the rulers, and the authorities, do not worry about how you are to defend yourselves or what you are to say;   12 for the Holy Spirit will teach you at that very hour what you ought to say."

12:13-14 Someone in the crowd said to him, "Teacher, tell my brother to divide the family inheritance with me."   14 But he said to him, "Friend, who set me to be a judge or arbitrator over you?"

12:16-21 Then he told them a parable: "The land of a rich man produced abundantly.   17 And he thought to himself, `What should I do, for I have no place to store my crops?'   18 Then he said, `I will do this: I will pull down my barns and build larger ones, and there I will store all my grain and my goods.   19 And I will say to my soul, `Soul, you have ample goods laid up for many years; relax, eat, drink, be merry.'   20 But God said to him, `You fool! This very night your life is being demanded of you. And the things you have prepared, whose will they be?'   21 So it is with those who store up treasures for themselves but are not rich toward God."

12:22-31 He said to his disciples, "Therefore I tell you, do not worry about your life, what you will eat, or about your body, what you will wear.   23 For life is more than food, and the body more than clothing.   24 Consider the ravens: they neither sow nor reap, they have neither storehouse nor barn, and yet God feeds them. Of how much more value are you than the birds!   25 And can any of you by worrying add a single hour to your span of life?   26 If then you are not able to do so small a thing as that, why do you worry about the rest? 27 Consider the lilies, how they grow: they neither toil nor spin; yet I tell you, even Solomon in all his glory was not clothed like one of these. 28 But if God so clothes the grass of the field, which is alive today and tomorrow is thrown into the oven, how much more will he clothe you-- you of little faith! 29 And do not keep striving for what you are to eat and what you are to drink, and do not keep worrying. 30 For it is the nations of the world that strive after all these things, and your Father knows that you need them. 31 Instead, strive for his kingdom, and these things will be given to you as well.

12:33-34 Sell your possessions, and give alms. Make purses for yourselves that do not wear out, an unfailing treasure in heaven, where no thief comes near and no moth destroys. 34 For where your treasure is, there your heart will be also.

12:39-40 "But know this: if the owner of the house had known at what hour the thief was coming, he would not have let his house be broken into. 40 You also must be ready, for the Son of Man is coming at an unexpected hour."

12:42-46 And the Lord said, "Who then is the faithful and prudent manager whom his master will put in charge of his slaves, to give them their allowance of food at the proper time? 43 Blessed is that slave whom his master will find at work when he arrives. 44 Truly I tell you, he will put that one in charge of all his possessions. 45

But if that slave says to himself, `My master is delayed in coming,' and if he begins to beat the other slaves, men and women, and to eat and drink and get drunk, 46 the master of that slave will come on a day when he does not expect him and at an hour that he does not know, and will cut him in pieces, and put him with the unfaithful.

12:49, 51-53 "I came to bring fire to the earth, and how I wish it were already kindled! 51 Do you think that I have come to bring peace to the earth? No, I tell you, but rather division! 52 From now on five in one household will be divided, three against two and two against three; 53 they will be divided: father against son and son against father, mother against daughter and daughter against mother, mother-in-law against her daughter-in-law and daughter-in-law against mother-in-law."

12:54-56 He also said to the crowds, "When you see a cloud rising in the west, you immediately say, `It is going to rain'; and so it happens. 55 And when you see the south wind blowing, you say, `There will be scorching heat'; and it happens. 56 You hypocrites! You know how to interpret the appearance of earth and sky, but why do you not know how to interpret the present time?

12:57-59 "And why do you not judge for yourselves what is right? 58 Thus, when you go with your accuser before a magistrate, on the way make an effort to settle the case, or you may be dragged before the judge, and the judge hand you over to the officer, and the officer throw you in prison. 59 I tell you, you will never get out until you have paid the very last penny."

13:18-21 He said therefore, "What is the kingdom of God like? And to what should I compare it? 19 It is like a mustard seed that someone took and sowed in the garden; it grew and became a tree, and the birds of the air made nests in its branches." 20 And again he said, "To what should I compare the kingdom of God? 21 It is like yeast that a woman took and mixed in with three measures of flour until all of it was leavened."

13:24-27 "Strive to enter through the narrow door; for many, I tell you, will try to enter and will not be able. 25 When once the owner of the house has got up and shut the door, and you begin to stand outside and to knock at the door, saying, `Lord, open to us,' then in reply he will say to you, `I do not know where you come from.' 26 Then you will begin to say, `We ate and drank with you, and you taught in our streets.' 27 But he will say, `I do not know where you come from; go away from me, all you evildoers!'

13:28-30 There will be weeping and gnashing of teeth when you see Abraham and Isaac and Jacob and all the prophets in the kingdom of God, and you yourselves thrown out. 29 Then people will come from east and west, from north and south, and will eat in the kingdom of God. 30 Indeed, some are last who will be first, and some are first who will be last."

13:34-35 Jerusalem, Jerusalem, the city that kills the prophets and stones those who are sent to it! How often have I desired to gather your children together as a hen gathers her brood under her wings, and you were not willing! 35 See, your house is left to you. And I tell you, you will not see me until the time comes when you say, `Blessed is the one who comes in the name of the Lord.'"

14:11, 18:14 For all who exalt themselves will be humbled, and those who humble themselves will be exalted."

18:14 I tell you, this man went down to his home justified rather than the other; for all who exalt themselves will be humbled, but all who humble themselves will be exalted."

14:16-24 Then Jesus said to him, "Someone gave a great dinner and invited many. 17 At the time for the dinner he sent his slave to say to those who had been invited, `Come; for everything is ready now.' 18 But they all alike began to make excuses. The first said to him, `I have bought a piece of land, and I must go out and see it; please accept my regrets.' 19 Another said, `I have bought five yoke of oxen, and I am going to try them out; please accept my regrets.' 20 Another said, `I have just been married, and therefore I cannot come.' 21 So the slave returned and reported this to his master. Then the owner of the house became angry and said to his slave, `Go out at once into the streets and lanes of the town and bring in the poor, the crippled, the blind, and the lame.' 22 And the slave said, `Sir, what you ordered has been done, and there is still room.' 23 Then the master said to the slave, `Go out into the roads and lanes, and compel people to come in, so that my house may be filled. 24 For I tell you, none of those who were invited will taste my dinner.'"

14:26-27, 17:33 "Whoever comes to me and does not hate father and mother, wife and children, brothers and sisters, yes, and even life itself, cannot be my disciple. 27 Whoever does not carry the cross and follow me cannot be my disciple.

17:33 Those who try to make their life secure will lose it, but those who lose their life will keep it.

14:34-35 "Salt is good; but if salt has lost its taste, how can its saltiness be restored? 35 It is fit neither for the soil nor for the manure pile; they throw it away. Let anyone with ears to hear listen!"

15:4-10 "Which one of you, having a hundred sheep and losing one of them, does not leave the ninety-nine in the wilderness and go after the one that is lost until he finds it? 5 When he has found it, he lays it on his shoulders and rejoices. 6 And when he comes home, he calls together his friends and neighbors, saying to them, `Rejoice with me, for I have found my sheep that was lost.' 7 Just so, I tell you, there will be more joy in heaven over one sinner who repents than over ninety-nine righteous persons who need no repentance. 8 "Or what woman having ten silver coins, if she loses one of them, does not light a lamp, sweep the house, and search carefully until she finds it? 9 When she has found it, she calls together her friends and neighbors, saying, `Rejoice with me, for I have found the coin that I had lost.' 10 Just so, I tell you, there is joy in the presence of the angels of God over one sinner who repents."

16:13 No slave can serve two masters; for a slave will either hate the one and love the other, or be devoted to the one and despise the other. You cannot serve God and wealth."

16:16 "The law and the prophets were in effect until John came; since then the good news of the kingdom of God is proclaimed, and everyone tries to enter it by force.

16:17 But it is easier for heaven and earth to pass away, than for one stroke of a letter in the law to be dropped.

16:18 "Anyone who divorces his wife and marries another commits adultery, and whoever marries a woman divorced from her husband commits adultery.

17:1-2 Jesus said to his disciples, "Occasions for stumbling are bound to come, but woe to anyone by whom they come! 2 It would be better for you if a millstone were hung around your neck and you were thrown into the sea than for you to cause one of these little ones to stumble.

17:3-4 Be on your guard! If another disciple sins, you must rebuke the offender, and if there is repentance, you must forgive. 4 And if the same person sins against you seven times a day, and turns back to you seven times and says, `I repent,' you must forgive."

17:6 The Lord replied, "If you had faith the size of a mustard seed, you could say to this mulberry tree, `Be uprooted and planted in the sea,' and it would obey you.

17:22-24, 26-30, 34-35, 37 Then he said to the disciples, "The days are coming when you will long to see one of the days of the Son of Man, and you will not see it. 23 They will say to you, `Look there!' or `Look here!' Do not go, do not set off in pursuit. 24 For as the lightning flashes and lights up the sky from one side to the other, so will the Son of Man be in his day. - 26 Just as it was in the days of Noah, so too it will be in the days of the Son of Man. 27 They were eating and drinking, and marrying and being given in marriage, until the day Noah entered the ark, and the flood came and destroyed all of them. 28 Likewise, just as it was in the days of Lot: they were eating and drinking, buying and selling, planting and building, 29 but on the day that Lot left Sodom, it rained fire and sulfur from heaven and destroyed all of them 30 -- it will be like that on the day that the Son of Man is revealed.

  34 I tell you, on that night there will be two in one bed; one will be taken and the other left. 35 There will be two women grinding meal together; one will be taken and the other left." - 37Then they

asked him, "Where, Lord?" He said to them, "Where the corpse is, there the vultures will gather."

19:12-26 So he said, "A nobleman went to a distant country to get royal power for himself and then return. 13 He summoned ten of his slaves, and gave them ten pounds, and said to them, `Do business with these until I come back.'  14 But the citizens of his country hated him and sent a delegation after him, saying, `We do not want this man to rule over us.' 15 When he returned, having received royal power, he ordered these slaves, to whom he had given the money, to be summoned so that he might find out what they had gained by trading. 16 The first came forward and said, `Lord, your pound has made ten more pounds.'  17 He said to him, `Well done, good slave! Because you have been trustworthy in a very small thing, take charge of ten cities.' 18 Then the second came, saying, `Lord, your pound has made five pounds.'  19 He said to him, `And you, rule over five cities.' 20 Then the other came, saying, `Lord, here is your pound. I wrapped it up in a piece of cloth,  21 for I was afraid of you, because you are a harsh man; you take what you did not deposit, and reap what you did not sow.'  22 He said to him, `I will judge you by your own words, you wicked slave! You knew, did you, that I was a harsh man, taking what I did not deposit and reaping what I did not sow? 23 Why then did you not put my money into the bank? Then when I returned, I could have collected it with interest.' 24 He said to the bystanders, `Take the pound from him and give it to the one who has ten pounds.'  25 (And they said to him, `Lord, he has ten

Before the Gospels

pounds!') 26 `I tell you, to all those who have, more will be given; but from those who have nothing, even what they have will be taken away.

22:28-30 "You are those who have stood by me in my trials; 29 and I confer on you, just as my Father has conferred on me, a kingdom, 30 so that you may eat and drink at my table in my kingdom, and you will sit on thrones judging the twelve tribes of Israel.

The Gospel of Thomas

In the winter of 1945, in Upper Egypt, an Arab peasant was gathering fertilizer and topsoil for his crops. While digging in the soft dirt he came across a large earthen vessel. Inside were scrolls containing hitherto unseen books.

The scrolls were discovered near the site of the ancient town of Chenoboskion, at the base of a mountain named Gebel et-Tarif, near Hamra-Dum, in the vicinity of Naj 'Hammadi, about sixty miles from Luxor in Egypt. The texts were written in the Coptic language and preserved on papyrus sheets. The lettering style dated them as having been penned around the third or fourth century A.D. The Gospel of Thomas is the longest of the volumes consisting of between 114 and 118 verses. Recent study indicates that the original works, of which the scrolls are copies, may predate the four canonical gospels of Matthew, Mark, Luke, and John. The origin of The Gospel of Thomas is now thought to be from the first or second century A.D.

The peasant boy who found this treasure stood to be rewarded greatly. This could have been the discovery of a lifetime for his family, but the boy had no idea what he had. He took the scrolls home, where his mother burned some as kindling. Others were sold to the black market antique dealers in Cairo. It would be years until they found their way into the hands of a scholar. Part of the thirteenth codex was smuggled from Egypt to America. In 1955 the existence of the codex had reached the ears of Gilles Quispel, a professor of religion and history in the Netherlands. The race was on to find and translate the scrolls.

The introduction of the collected sayings of Jesus refers to the writer as "Didymus (Jude) Thomas." This is the same Thomas who doubted Jesus and was then told to place his hand within the breach in the side of the Savior. In the Gospel of St. John, he is referred to as "Didymus," which means "twin" in Greek. In Aramaic, the name "Jude" (or Judas) also carries the sense of "twin". The use of this title led some in the apocryphal tradition to believe that he was the brother and confidant of Jesus. However, when applied to Jesus himself, the literal meaning of "twin" must be rejected by orthodox Christianity as well as anyone adhering to the doctrine of the virgin birth of the only begotten son of God. The title is likely meant to signify that Thomas was a close confidant of Jesus.

Ancient church historians mention that Thomas preached to the Parthians in Persia and it is said he was buried in Edessa. Fourth century chronicles attribute the evangelization of India (Asia-Minor or Central Asia) to Thomas.

The text, which some believe predate the four gospels, has a more Eastern flavor than the other gospels. Since it is widely held that the four gospels of Matthew, Mark, and Luke have a common reference in the basic text of Mark, it stands to reason that all follow the same general insight and language. Since scholars believe that the Gospel of Thomas predates the four main gospels, it can be assumed it was written outside the influences common to the other gospels. Although the codex found in Egypt is dated to the fourth century, the actual construction of the text of Thomas is placed by most Biblical scholars at about 50 to 70 A.D. with a few scholars pushing the date out to 150 A.D.

If Thomas wrote his gospel first, without input from Mark, and from the standpoint of Eastern exposure as a result of his sojourn into India, it could explain the "Eastern" quality of the text.

Moreover, there is some speculation that the sayings found in Thomas could be more accurate to the original intent and wording of Jesus than the other gospels. This may seem counter-intuitive until we realize that Christianity itself is an Eastern religion, albeit Middle-Eastern. Although, as it spread west the faith went through many changes to westernize or Romanize it...Jesus was both mystical and Middle-Eastern.

The Gospel of Thomas was most likely composed in Syria, where tradition holds the church of Edessa was founded by Judas Thomas, "The Twin" (Didymus). The gospel may well be the earliest written tradition in the Syriac church

The Gospel of Thomas is sometimes called a Gnostic gospel. The term "Gnostic" derives from "gnosis," which in Greek means "knowledge." Gnostics believed that knowledge is formed or found from a personal encounter with God brought about by inward or intuitive insight. They believed they were privy to a secret knowledge about the divine. It is this knowledge that leads to their name. It is possible that the roots of the Gnostic system pre-dates Christianity and found a suitable home in the mystical side of the Christian faith.

There are numerous references to the Gnostics in second century literature. Their form of Christianity was considered heresy by the early church fathers. It is from the writings condemning the group that we glean most of our information. They are alluded to in the Bible in 1 Tm 1:4 and 1 Tm 6:20, and possibly the entirety of Jude, as the writers of the Bible defended their theology against that of the Gnostics.

The relation between the Gospel of Thomas and the Q document is an interesting one.

The Gospel of Thomas is very different from the gospels that have become part of the New Testament. Like Q, it contains no narrative material, nor is there any story of the birth, the life, or the death of Jesus. It consists only of sayings, 114 in all. The Gospel of Thomas makes a claim in the first page of the text announcing that it is the words of the "living Jesus. The gospel contains the same basic information as Q1 and Q2 of the "three evolutionary stages of Q" hypothesis.

Some of the sayings from the Gospel of Thomas are very much like those found in the gospels of Matthew and Luke.

For New Testament scholars, one of the most interesting things about this gospel is that its author (who calls himself Didymos Judas Thomas) appears to have used sayings from the same collection used by Matthew and Luke. Thus, the Gospel of Thomas may be proof of a central and core collection of sayings directly from the mouth of Jesus. There may have been a small number of these collection, which may have varied slightly in wording and in which sayings were recorded but the source material would have come from Jesus himself. Since the wording of the sayings in Matthew, Mark, Luke, and Thomas were so similar it solidified the belief by some scholars of a center repository of information.

Before the Gospels

In 1989, a team of researchers led by James M. Robinson of the Institute for Antiquity and Christianity in Claremont, CA, began the "reconstruction" of the Gospel of Q. Robinson and his team are accomplishing this by a highly detailed literary analysis of Matthew, Luke, and Thomas. Their painstaking work goes verse by verse, word by word. Since this respected team has seen fit to use the Gospel of Thomas as part of the collected works for the reconstruction of Q, it may benefit us to examine this book also. As we will see, Thomas, like Q1 and Q2, did not see Jesus in the same light of divinity as Paul and the later Christian movement casts him in.

Based on the fact that there was simply a collection of sayings, which predated the narratives of the resurrection, and based on what those saying were, we can conclude that some Christian communities did not see Jesus as a Messiah. Jesus was not divine, but fully human. To them Jesus was a teacher of wisdom, a man who tried to teach others how to live. The story of the resurrection may have developed a little later in the evolution of the faith and the passion narrative was added to the collection of sayings to yield the gospel we have today.

We have seen the Q collection. Now let us compare it to the sayings collected by Thomas.

The Gospel Of Thomas

These are the secret sayings which the living Jesus has spoken and Judas who is also Thomas (the twin) (Didymos Judas Thomas) wrote.

1. And he said: Whoever finds the interpretation of these sayings will not taste death.

John 8:51 Very truly I tell you, whoever keeps my word will never see death.

2. Jesus said: Let he who seeks not stop seeking until he finds, and when he finds he will be troubled, and when he has been troubled he will marvel (be astonished) and he will reign over all and in reigning, he will find rest.

3. Jesus said: If those who lead you say to you: Behold, the Kingdom is in the sky, then the birds of the sky would enter before you. If they say to you: It is in the sea, then the fish of the

sea would enter ahead you. But the Kingdom of God exists within you and it exists outside of you. Those who come to know (recognize) themselves will find it, and when you come to know yourselves you will become known and you will realize that you are the children of the Living Father. Yet if you do not come to know yourselves then you will dwell in poverty and it will be you who are that poverty.

Luke 17:20 And when he was demanded of by the Pharisees, when the kingdom of God should come, he answered them and said, The kingdom of God cometh not with observation: Neither shall they say, Lo here! Lo There! For, behold, the kingdom of God is within you.

4. Jesus said: The person of old age will not hesitate to ask a little child of seven days about the place of life, and he will live. For many who are first will become last, (and the last will be first). And they will become one and the same.

Mark 9:35 He sat down, called the twelve, and said to them: Whoever wants to be first must be last of all and servant of all. 36 Then he took a little child and put it among them, and taking it in his arms, he said to them: 37 Whoever welcomes one such child in my name welcomes me, and whoever welcomes me welcomes not me but the one who sent me.

5. Jesus said: Recognize what is in front of your face, and what has been hidden from you will be revealed to you. For there is nothing hidden which will not be revealed (become manifest), and nothing buried that will not be raised.

Mark 4:2 For there is nothing hid, except to be made manifest; nor is anything secret, except to come to light.

Luke 12:3 Nothing is covered up that will not be revealed, or hidden that will not be known.

Matthew 10:26 So have no fear of them; for nothing is covered up that will not be uncovered, and nothing secret that will not become known.

6. His Disciples asked Him, how do you want us to fast, and how will we pray? And how will we be charitable (give alms), and what laws of diet will we maintain?

Jesus said: Do not lie, and do not practice what you hate, for everything is in the plain sight of Heaven. For there is nothing concealed that will not become manifest, and there is nothing covered that will not be exposed.

Before the Gospels

Luke 11:1 *He was praying in a certain place, and after he had finished, one of his disciples said to him, Lord, teach us to pray, as John taught his disciples.*

7. Jesus said: Blessed is the lion that the man will eat, for the lion will become the man. Cursed is the man that the lion shall eat, and still the lion will become man.

Mathew 26:20-30 *He who dipped his hand with me in the dish, the same will betray me. The Son of Man goes, even as it is written of him, but woe to that man through whom the Son of Man is betrayed! It would be better for that man if he had not been born. Judas, who betrayed him, answered, It isn't me, is it, Rabbi? He said to him, You said it. As they were eating, Jesus took bread, gave thanks for it, and broke it. He gave to the disciples, and said, Take, eat; this is my body. He took the cup, gave thanks, and gave to them, saying: All of you drink it, for this is my blood of the new covenant, which is poured out for many for the remission of sins. But I tell you that I will not drink of this fruit of the vine from now on, until that day when I drink it anew with you in my Father's Kingdom. When they had sung a hymn, they went out to the Mount of Olives.*

8. And he said: The Kingdom of Heaven is like a wise fisherman who casts his net into the sea. He drew it up from the sea full of small fish. Among them he found a fine large fish. That wise

fisherman threw all the small fish back into the sea and chose the large fish without hesitation. Whoever has ears to hear, let him hear!

Matthew 13:47 Again, the kingdom of heaven is like a net that was thrown into the sea and caught fish of every kind; 48 when it was full, they drew it ashore, sat down, and put the good into baskets but threw out the bad.

9. Jesus said: Now, the sower came forth. He filled his hand and threw (the seeds). Some fell upon the road and the birds came and gathered them up. Others fell on the stone and they did not take deep enough roots in the soil, and so did not produce grain. Others fell among the thorns and they choked the seed, and the worm ate them. Others fell upon the good earth and it produced good fruit up toward the sky, it bore 60 fold and 120 fold.

Matthew 13:3 And he told them many things in parables, saying: Listen! A sower went out to sow. 4 And as he sowed, some seeds fell on the path, and the birds came and ate them up. 5 Other seeds fell on rocky ground, where they did not have much soil, and they sprang up quickly, since they had no depth of soil. 6 But when the sun rose, they were scorched; and since they had no root, they withered away. 7 Other seeds fell among thorns, and the thorns grew up and choked them. 8 Other seeds fell on good soil and brought forth grain, some a hundredfold, some sixty, some thirty.

Before the Gospels

Mark 4:2 And he taught them many things in parables, and in his teaching he said to them: 3 Behold! A sower went out to sow. 4 And as he sowed, some seed fell along the path, and the birds came and devoured it. 5 Other seed fell on rocky ground, where it had not much soil, and immediately it sprang up, since it had no depth of soil; 6 and when the sun rose it was scorched, and since it had no root it withered away. 7 Other seed fell among thorns and the thorns grew up and choked it, and it yielded no grain. 8 And other seeds fell into good soil and brought forth grain, growing up and increasing and yielding thirty fold and sixty fold and a hundredfold. 9 And he said, He who has ears to hear, let him hear.

Luke 8:4 And when a great crowd came together and people from town after town came to him, he said in a parable: 5 A sower went out to sow his seed; and as he sowed, some fell along the path, and was trodden under foot, and the birds of the air devoured it. 6 And some fell on the rock; and as it grew up, it withered away, because it had no moisture. 7 And some fell among thorns; and the thorns grew with it and choked it. 8 And some fell into good soil and grew, and yielded a hundredfold. As he said this, he called out, He who has ears to hear, let him hear.

10. Jesus said: I have cast fire upon the world and behold, I guard it until it is ablaze.

Luke 12:49 I came to bring fire to the earth, and how I wish it were already kindled.

11. Jesus said: This sky will pass away, and the one above it will pass away. The dead are not alive, and the living will not die. In the days when you consumed what is dead, you made it alive. When you come into the Light, what will you do? On the day when you were united (one), you became separated (two). When you have become separated (two), what will you do?

Matthew 24:35 Heaven and earth will pass away, but my words will not pass away.

12. The Disciples said to Jesus: We know that you will go away from us. Who is it that will be our teacher?

Jesus said to them: Wherever you are (in the place that you have come), you will go to James the Righteous, for whose sake Heaven and Earth were made (came into being).

13. Jesus said to his Disciples: Compare me to others, and tell me who I am like. Simon Peter said to him: You are like a righteous messenger (angel) of God. Matthew said to him: You are like a (wise) philosopher (of the heart). Thomas said to him: Teacher, my mouth is not capable of saying who you are like!

Jesus said: I'm not your teacher, now that you have drunk; you have become drunk from the bubbling spring that I have tended (measured out). And he took him, and withdrew and spoke three words to him: "ahyh ashr ahyh" (I am Who I am).

Now when Thomas returned to his comrades, they inquired of him: What did Jesus say to you? Thomas said to them: If I tell you even one of the words which he spoke to me, you will take up stones and throw them at me, and fire will come from the stones to consume you.

Mark 8:27 Jesus went on with his disciples to the villages of Caesarea Philippi; and on the way he asked his disciples, Who do people say that I am? 28 And they answered him, John the Baptist; and others, Elijah; and still others, one of the prophets. 29 He asked them, But who do you say that I am? Peter answered him, You are the Messiah. 30 And he sternly ordered them not to tell anyone about him.

14. Jesus said to them: If you fast, you will give rise to transgression (sin) for yourselves. And if you pray, you will be condemned. And if you give alms, you will cause harm (evil) to your spirits. And when you go into the countryside, if they take you in (receive you) then eat what they set before you and heal

the sick among them. For what goes into your mouth will not defile you, but rather what comes out of your mouth, that is what will defile you.

Luke 10:8 Whenever you enter a town and its people welcome you, eat what is set before you; 9 Cure the sick who are there, and say to them, The kingdom of God has come near to you.

Mark 7:15 There is nothing outside a person that by going in can defile, but the things that come out are what defile.

Matthew 15:11 Not that what goes into the mouth defiles a man, but what comes out of the mouth, this defiles a man.
Romans 14.14 I know and am persuaded in the Lord Jesus that nothing is unclean in itself; but it is unclean for any one who thinks it unclean.

15. Jesus said: When you see him who was not born of woman, bow yourselves down upon your faces and worship him for he is your Father.

16. Jesus said: People think perhaps I have come to spread peace upon the world. They do not know that I have come to cast dissention (conflict) upon the earth; fire, sword, war. For there will be five in a house. Three will be against two and two against

three, the father against the son and the son against the father. And they will stand alone.

Matthew 10:34 Do not think that I have come to bring peace to the earth; I have not come to bring peace, but a sword. 35 For I have come to set a man against his father, and a daughter against her mother, and a daughter-in-law against her mother-in-law; 36 and one's foes will be members of one's own household.

Luke 12:51 Do you think that I have come to give peace on earth? No, I tell you, but rather division; 52 for henceforth in one house there will be five divided, three against two and two against three; 53 they will be divided, father against son and son against father, mother against daughter and daughter against her mother, mother-in-law against her daughter-in-law and daughter-in-law against her mother-in-law.

17. Jesus said: I will give to you what eye has not seen, what ear has not heard, what hand has not touched, and what has not occurred to the mind of man.

1 Cor 2:9 But, as it is written, What no eye has seen, nor ear heard, nor the human heart conceived, what God has prepared for those who love him.

18. The Disciples said to Jesus: Tell us how our end will come. Jesus said: Have you already discovered the beginning (origin), so that you inquire about the end? Where the beginning (origin) is, there the end will be. Blessed be he who will take his place in the beginning (stand at the origin) for he will know the end, and he will not experience death.

19. Jesus said: Blessed is he who came into being before he came into being. If you become my Disciples and heed my sayings, these stones will serve you. For there are five trees in paradise for you, which are undisturbed in summer and in winter and their leaves do not fall. Whoever knows them will not experience death.

20. The Disciples said to Jesus: Tell us what the Kingdom of Heaven is like. He said to them: It is like a mustard seed, smaller than all other seeds and yet when it falls on the tilled earth, it produces a great plant and becomes shelter for the birds of the sky.

Mark 4:30 He also said, With what can we compare the kingdom of God, or what parable will we use for it? 31 It is like a mustard seed, which, when sown upon the ground, is the smallest of all the seeds on earth; 32 yet when

Before the Gospels

it is sown it grows up and becomes the greatest of all shrubs, and puts forth large branches, so that the birds of the air can make nests in its shade. Matthew 13:31 The kingdom of heaven is like a grain of mustard seed which a man took and sowed in his field; 32 it is the smallest of all seeds, but when it has grown it is the greatest of shrubs and becomes a tree, so that the birds of the air come and make nests in its branches.

Luke 13.18 He said therefore, What is the kingdom of God like? And to what shall I compare it? 19 It is like a grain of mustard seed which a man took and sowed in his garden; and it grew and became a tree, and the birds of the air made nests in its branches.

21. Mary said to Jesus: Who are your Disciples like? He said: They are like little children who are living in a field that is not theirs. When the owners of the field come, they will say: Let us have our field! It is as if they were naked in front of them (They undress in front of them in order to let them have what is theirs) and they give back the field. Therefore I said, if the owner of the house knows that the thief is coming, he will be alert before he arrives and will not allow him to dig through into the house to carry away his belongings. You must be on guard and beware of the world (system). Prepare yourself (arm yourself) with great strength or the bandits will find a way to reach you, for the problems you expect will come. Let there be among you a person of understanding (awareness). When the crop ripened, he came quickly with his sickle in his hand to reap. Whoever has ears to hear, let him hear!

Matthew 24:43 But understand this: if the owner of the house had known in what part of the night the thief was coming, he would have stayed awake and would not have let his house be broken into.

Mark 4:26 He also said, The kingdom of God is as if someone would scatter seed on the ground, 27 and would sleep and rise night and day, and the seed would sprout and grow, he does not know how. 28 The earth produces of itself, first the stalk, then the head, then the full grain in the head. 29 But when the grain is ripe, at once he goes in with his sickle, because the harvest has come.

Luke 12:39 But know this, that if the householder had known at what hour the thief was coming, he would not have left his house to be broken into. 40 You also must be ready; for the Son of man is coming at an unexpected hour.

22. Jesus saw little children who were being suckled. He said to his Disciples: These little children who are being suckled are like those who enter the Kingdom.

They said to him: Should we become like little children in order to enter the Kingdom?

Jesus said to them: When you make the two one, and you make the inside as the outside and the outside as the inside, when you make the above as the below, and if you make the male and the female one and the same (united male and female) so that the man will not be masculine (male) and the female be not feminine (female), when you establish an eye in the place of an eye and a hand in the place of a hand and a foot in the place of a foot and an likeness (image) in the place of a likeness (an image), then will you enter the Kingdom.

Luke 18:16 But Jesus called for them and said, Let the little children come to me, and do not stop them; for it is to such as these that the kingdom of God belongs. 17 Truly I tell you, whoever does not receive the kingdom of God as a little child will never enter it.

Mark 9:43 If your hand causes you to stumble, cut it off; it is better for you to enter life maimed than to have two hands and to go to hell, to the unquenchable fire. 45 And if your foot causes you to stumble, cut it off; it is better for you to enter life lame than to have two feet and to be thrown into hell. 47 And if your eye causes you to stumble, tear it out; it is better for you to enter the kingdom of God with one eye than to have two eyes and to be thrown into hell, 48 where their worm never dies, and the fire is never quenched.

Matthew 18:3 And said, Verily, I say unto you, unless you turn and become like children, you will never enter the kingdom of heaven. 4

Whoever humbles himself like this child, he is the greatest in the kingdom of heaven. 5 Whoever receives one such child in my name receives me;

Matthew 5:29 If your right eye causes you to sin, pluck it out and throw it away; it is better that you lose one of your members than that your whole body be thrown into hell. 30 And if your right hand causes you to sin, cut it off and throw it away; it is better that you lose one of your members than that your whole body go into hell.

23. Jesus said: I will choose you, one out of a thousand and two out of ten thousand and they will stand as a single one.

24. His Disciples said: Show us the place where you are (your place), for it is necessary for us to seek it.

He said to them: Whoever has ears, let him hear! Within a man of light there is light, and he illumines the entire world. If he does not shine, he is darkness (there is darkness).

John13:36 Simon Peter said to him, Lord, where are you going? Jesus answered, Where I am going, you cannot follow me now; but you will follow afterward.

Matthew 6:22 The eye is the lamp of the body. So, if your eye is healthy, your whole body will be full of light; 23 but if your eye is unhealthy, your whole body will be full of darkness. If then the light in you is darkness, how great is the darkness!

Luke 11:34 Your eye is the lamp of your body; when your eye is sound, your whole body is full of light; but when it is not sound, your body is full of darkness. 35 Therefore be careful lest the light in you be darkness. 36 If then your whole body is full of light, having no part dark, it will be wholly bright, as when a lamp with its rays gives you light.

25. Jesus said: Love your friend (Brother) as your soul; protect him as you would the pupil of your own eye.

26. Jesus said: You see the speck in your brother's eye but the beam that is in your own eye you do not see. When you remove the beam out of your own eye, then will you see clearly to remove the speck out of your brother's eye.

Matthew 7:3 Why do you see the speck in your neighbor's eye, but do not notice the log in your own eye? 4 Or how can you say to your neighbor, Let me take the speck out of your eye, while the log is in your own eye? 5 You hypocrite, first take the log out of your own eye, and then you will see clearly to take the speck out of your neighbor's eye.

Luke 6:41 Why do you see the speck that is in your brother's eye, but do not notice the log that is in your own eye? 42 Or how can you say to your brother, Brother, let me take out the speck that is in your eye, when you yourself do not see the log that is in your own eye? You hypocrite, first take the log out of your own eye, and then you will see clearly to take out the speck that is in your brother's eye.

27. Jesus said: Unless you fast from the world (system), you will not find the Kingdom of God. Unless you keep the Sabbath (entire week) as Sabbath, you will not see the Father.

28. Jesus said: I stood in the midst of the world. In the flesh I appeared to them. I found them all drunk; I found none thirsty among them. My soul grieved for the sons of men, for they are blind in their hearts and do not see that they came into the world empty, they are destined (determined) to leave the world empty. However, now they are drunk. When they have shaken off their wine, then they will repent (change their ways).

29. Jesus said: If the flesh came into being because of spirit, it is a marvel, but if spirit came into being because of the body, it would be a marvel of marvels. I marvel indeed at how great wealth has taken up residence in this poverty.

30. Jesus said: Where there are three gods, they are gods (Where there are three gods they are without god). Where there is only one, I say that I am with him. Lift the stone and there you will find me, Split the wood and there am I.

Matthew 18:20 For where two or three are gathered in my name, I am there among them.

31. Jesus said: No prophet is accepted in his own village, no physician heals those who know him.

Mark 6:4 Then Jesus said to them, Prophets are not without honor, except in their hometown, and among their own kin, and in their own house.

Matthew 13:57 And they took offense at him. But Jesus said to them: A prophet is not without honor save in his own country and in his own house.

Luke 4:24 And he said, Truly, I say to you, no prophet is acceptable in his own country.

John 4:43 After the two days he departed to Galilee. 44 For Jesus himself testified that a prophet has no honor in his own country.

32. Jesus said: A city being built (and established) upon a high mountain and fortified cannot fall nor can it be hidden.

Matthew 5:14 You are the light of the world. A city built on a hill cannot be hid.

33. Jesus said: What you will hear in your ear preach from your rooftops. For no one lights a lamp and sets it under a basket nor puts it in a hidden place, but rather it is placed upon a lamp-stand so that everyone who comes and goes will see its light.

Matthew 10:27 What I say to you in the dark, tell in the light; and what you hear whispered, proclaim from the housetops.

Luke 8:16 No one after lighting a lamp hides it under a jar, or puts it under a bed, but puts it on a lamp stand, so that those who enter may see the light.

Matthew 5:15 Nor do men light a lamp and put it under a bushel, but on a stand, and it gives light to all in the house.

Before the Gospels

Mark 4:21 *And he said to them, Is a lamp brought in to be put under a bushel, or under a bed, and not on a stand?*

Luke 11:33 *No one after lighting a lamp puts it in a cellar or under a bushel, but on a stand, that those who enter may see the light.*

34. Jesus said: If a blind person leads a blind person, both fall into a pit.

Matthew 15:14 *Let them alone; they are blind guides of the blind. And if one blind person guides another, both will fall into a pit.*
Luke 6:39 *He also told them a parable: Can a blind man lead a blind man? Will they not both fall into a pit?*

35. Jesus said: It is impossible for anyone to enter the house of a strong man to take it by force unless he binds his hands, then he will be able to loot his house.

Matthew 12:29 *Or how can one enter a strong man's house and plunder his goods, unless he first binds the strong man? Then indeed he may plunder his house.*

Luke 11:21 When a strong man, fully armed, guards his own palace, his goods are in peace; 22 but when one stronger than he assails him and overcomes him, he takes away his armor in which he trusted, and divides his spoil.

Mark 3:27 But no one can enter a strong man's house and plunder his property without first tying up the strong man; then indeed the house can be plundered.

36. Jesus said: Do not worry from morning to evening nor from evening to morning about the food that you will eat nor about what clothes you will wear. You are much superior to the lilies which neither card nor spin. When you have no clothing, what do you wear? Who can add time to your life (increase your stature)? He himself will give to you your garment.

Matthew 6:25 Therefore I tell you, do not worry about your life, what you will eat or what you will drink, or about your body, what you will wear. Is not life more than food, and the body more than clothing? 26 Look at the birds of the air; they neither sow nor reap nor gather into barns, and yet your heavenly Father feeds them. Are you not of more value than they? 27 And can any of you by worrying add a single hour to your span of life? 28 And why do you worry about clothing? Consider the lilies of the field, how they grow; they neither toil nor spin, 29 yet I tell you, even Solomon in all his glory was not clothed like one of these. 30 But if God so clothes the grass of the field, which is alive today and tomorrow is thrown into the oven, will he not much more clothe you--you of little faith? 31 Therefore do not worry, saying, What will we eat? or What will we drink? or What will we wear?

Luke 12:22 And he said to his disciples, Therefore I tell you, do not be anxious about your life, what you shall eat, nor about your body, what you shall put on. 23 For life is more than food, and the body more than clothing.

37. His Disciples said: When will you appear to us, and when will we see you?

Jesus said: When you take off your garments without being ashamed, and place your garments under your feet and tread on them as the little children do, then will you see the Son of the Living-One, and you will not be afraid.

38. Jesus said: Many times have you yearned to hear these sayings which I speak to you, and you have no one else from whom to hear them. There will be days when you will seek me but you will not find me.

39. Jesus said: The Pharisees and the Scribes have received the keys of knowledge, but they have hidden them. They did not go in, nor did they permit those who wished to enter to do so. However, you be as wise (astute) as serpents and innocent as doves.

Luke 11:52 Woe to you lawyers! For you have taken away the key of knowledge; you did not enter yourselves, and you hindered those who were entering.

Matthew 10:16 See, I am sending you out like sheep into the midst of wolves; so be wise as serpents and innocent as doves.

Matthew 23.13 But woe unto you, scribes and Pharisees, hypocrites! because you shut the kingdom of heaven against men; for you neither enter yourselves, nor allow those who would enter to go in.

40. Jesus said: A grapevine has been planted outside the (vineyard of the) Father, and since it is not viable (supported) it will be pulled up by its roots and destroyed.

Matthew 15:13 He answered, Every plant that my heavenly Father has not planted will be uprooted.

41. Jesus said: Whoever has (it) in his hand, to him will (more) be given. And whoever does not have, from him will be taken even the small amount which he has.

Matthew 25:29 For to all those who have, more will be given, and they will have an abundance; but from those who have nothing, even what they have will be taken away.

Luke 19:26 I tell you, that to every one who has will more be given; but from him who has not, even what he has will be taken away.

42. Jesus said: Become passers-by.

43. His Disciples said to him: Who are you, that you said these things to us?

Jesus said to them: You do not recognize who I am from what I said to you, but rather you have become like the Jews who either love the tree and hate its fruit, or love the fruit and hate the tree.

John 8:25 They said to him, Who are you? Jesus said to them, Why do I speak to you at all?

Matthew 7:16 You will know them by their fruits. Are grapes gathered from thorns, or figs from thistles? 17 In the same way, every good tree bears good fruit, but the bad tree bears bad fruit. 18 A good tree cannot bear bad fruit, nor can a bad tree bear good fruit. 19 Every tree that does not bear good fruit is cut down and thrown into the fire. 20 Thus you will know them by their fruits.

44. Jesus said: Whoever blasphemes against the Father, it will be forgiven him. And whoever blasphemes against the Son, it will be forgiven him. Yet whoever blasphemes against the Holy Spirit, it will not be forgiven him neither on earth nor in heaven.

Mark 3:28 Truly I tell you, people will be forgiven for their sins and whatever blasphemies they utter; 29 but whoever blasphemes against the Holy Spirit can never have forgiveness, but is guilty of an eternal sin.

Matthew 12:31 Therefore I tell you, every sin and blasphemy will be forgiven men, but the blasphemy against the Spirit will not be forgiven. 32 And whoever says a word against the Son of man will be forgiven; but whoever speaks against the Holy Spirit will not be forgiven, either in this age or in the age to come.

Before the Gospels

Luke 12:10 And every one who speaks a word against the Son of man will be forgiven; but he who blasphemes against the Holy Spirit will not be forgiven.

45. Jesus said: Grapes are not harvested from thorns, nor are figs gathered from thistles, for they do not give fruit. A good person brings forth goodness out of his storehouse. A bad person brings forth evil out of his evil storehouse which is in his heart, and he speaks evil, for out of the abundance of the heart he brings forth evil.

Luke 6:43 For no good tree bears bad fruit, nor again does a bad tree bear good fruit; 44 for each tree is known by its own fruit. For figs are not gathered from thorns, nor are grapes picked from a bramble bush. 45 The good man out of the good treasure of his heart produces good, and the evil man out of his evil treasure produces evil; for out of the abundance of the heart his mouth speaks.

46. Jesus said: From Adam until John the Baptist there is none born of women who surpasses John the Baptist, so that his eyes should not be downcast (lowered). Yet I have said that whoever among you becomes like a child will know the Kingdom, and he will be greater than John.

Matthew 11:11 Truly I tell you, among those born of women no one has arisen greater than John the Baptist; yet the least in the kingdom of heaven is greater than he.

Luke 7:28 I tell you, among those born of women none is greater than John; yet he who is least in the kingdom of God is greater than he.

Matthew 18:2 He called a child, whom he put among them, 3 and said, Truly I tell you, unless you change and become like children, you will never enter the kingdom of heaven. 18:4 Whoever becomes humble like this child is the greatest in the kingdom of heaven.

47. Jesus said: It is impossible for a man to mount two horses or to draw two bows, and a servant cannot serve two masters, otherwise he will honor the one and disrespect the other. No man drinks vintage wine and immediately desires to drink new wine, and they do not put new wine into old wineskins or they would burst, and they do not put vintage wine into new wineskins or it would spoil (sour). They do not sew an old patch on a new garment because that would cause a split.

Matthew 6:24 No one can serve two masters; for a slave will either hate the one and love the other, or be devoted to the one and despise the other. You cannot serve God and wealth.

Before the Gospels

Matthew 9:16 No one sews a piece of unshrunk cloth on an old cloak, for the patch pulls away from the cloak, and a worse tear is made. 17 Neither is new wine put into old wineskins; otherwise, the skins burst, and the wine is spilled, and the skins are destroyed; but new wine is put into fresh wineskins, and so both are preserved.

Mark 2:21 No one sews a piece of unshrunk cloth on an old garment; if he does, the patch tears away from it, the new from the old, and a worse tear is made. 22 And no one puts new wine into old wineskins; if he does, the wine will burst the skins, and the wine is lost, and so are the skins; but new wine is for fresh skins.

Luke 5:36 He told them a parable also: No one tears a piece from a new garment and puts it upon an old garment; if he does, he will tear the new, and the piece from the new will not match the old. 37 And no one puts new wine into old wineskins; if he does, the new wine will burst the skins and it will be spilled, and the skins will be destroyed. 38 But new wine must be put into fresh wineskins. 39 And no one after drinking old wine desires new; for he says, The old is good.

48. Jesus said: If two make peace with each other in this one house, they will say to the mountain: Be moved! and it will be moved.

Matthew 18:19 Again, truly I tell you, if two of you agree on earth about anything you ask, it will be done for you by my Father in heaven.

Mark 11:23 Truly I tell you, if you say to this mountain, Be taken up and thrown into the sea, and if you do not doubt in your heart, but believe that what you say will come to pass, it will be done for you. 24 So I tell you, whatever you ask for in prayer, believe that you have received it, and it will be yours.

Matthew 17:20 He said to them, Because of your little faith. For truly, I say to you, if you have faith as a grain of mustard seed, you will say to this mountain, Move from here to there, and it will move; and nothing will be impossible to you.

49. Jesus said: Blessed is the solitary and chosen, for you will find the Kingdom. You have come from it, and unto it you will return.

50. Jesus said: If they say to you: From where do you come? Say to them: We have come from the Light, the place where the Light came into existence of its own accord and he stood and appeared in their image. If they say to you: Is it you? (Who are you?), say: We are his Sons and we are the chosen of the Living Father. If they ask you: What is the sign of your Father in you? Say to them: It is movement with rest. (Peace in the midst of motion.)

Before the Gospels

51. His Disciples said to him: When will the rest of the dead occur, and when will the New World come? He said to them: That which you look for has already come, but you do not recognize it.

52. His Disciples said to him: Twenty-four prophets preached in Israel, and they all spoke of (in) you. He said to them: You have ignored the Living-One who is in your presence and you have spoken only of the dead.

53. His Disciples said to him: Is circumcision beneficial or not? He said to them: If it were beneficial, their father would beget them already circumcised from their mother. However, the true spiritual circumcision has become entirely beneficial.

54. Jesus said: Blessed be the poor, for yours is the Kingdom of the Heaven.

Matthew 6:20 Then he looked up at his disciples and said: Blessed are you who are poor, for yours is the kingdom of God.

Luke 6:20 And he lifted up his eyes on his disciples, and said: Blessed are you poor, for yours is the kingdom of God.

Matthew 5:3 Blessed are the poor in spirit, for theirs is the kingdom of heaven.

55. Jesus said: Whoever does not hate his father and his mother will not be able to become my Disciple. And whoever does not hate his brothers and his sisters and does not take up his own cross in my way, will not become worthy of me.

Matthew 10:37 Whoever loves father or mother more than me is not worthy of me; and whoever loves son or daughter more than me is not worthy of me; 38 and whoever does not take up the cross and follow me is not worthy of me.

Luke 14:26 If any one comes to me and does not hate his own father and mother and wife and children and brothers and sisters, yes, and even his own life, he cannot be my disciple. 27 Whoever does not bear his own cross and come after me, cannot be my disciple.

56. Jesus said: Whoever has come to understand the world (system) has found a corpse, and whoever has found a corpse, is superior to the world (of him the system is not worthy).

57. Jesus said: The Kingdom of the Father is like a person who has good seed. His enemy came by night and sowed a

weed among the good seed. The man did not permit them to pull up the weed, he said to them: perhaps you will intend to pull up the weed and you pull up the wheat along with it. But, on the day of harvest the weeds will be very visible and then they will pull them and burn them.

Matthew 13:24 He put before them another parable: The kingdom of heaven may be compared to someone who sowed good seed in his field; 25 but while everybody was asleep, an enemy came and sowed weeds among the wheat, and then went away. 26 So when the plants came up and bore grain, then the weeds appeared as well. 27 And the slaves of the householder came and said to him, Master, did you not sow good seed in your field? Where, then, did these weeds come from? 28 He answered, An enemy has done this. The slaves said to him, Then do you want us to go and gather them? 29 But he replied, No; for in gathering the weeds you would uproot the wheat along with them. 30 Let both of them grow together until the harvest; and at harvest time I will tell the reapers, Collect the weeds first and bind them in bundles to be burned, but gather the wheat into my barn.

58. Jesus said: Blessed is the person who has suffered, for he has found life. (Blessed is he who has suffered [to find life] and found life).

Matthew 11:28 Come to me, all you that are weary and are carrying heavy burdens, and I will give you rest.

59. Jesus said: Look to the Living-One while you are alive, otherwise, you might die and seek to see him and will be unable to find him.

John 7:34 You will search for me, but you will not find me; and where I am, you cannot come.

John 13:33 Little children, I am with you only a little longer. You will look for me; and as I said to the Jews so now I say to you, Where I am going, you cannot come.

60. They saw a Samaritan carrying a lamb, on his way to Judea. Jesus said to them: Why does he take the lamb with him? They said to him: So that he may kill it and eat it. He said to them: While it is alive he will not eat it, but only after he kills it and it becomes a corpse. They said: How could he do otherwise? He said to them: Look for a place of rest for yourselves, otherwise, you might become corpses and be eaten.

61. Jesus said: Two will rest on a bed and one will die and the other will live. Salome said: Who are you, man? As if sent by

someone, you laid upon my bed and you ate from my table. Jesus said to her: "I-Am" he who is from that which is whole (the undivided). I have been given the things of my Father. Salome said: I am your Disciple. Jesus said to her: Thus, I say that whenever someone is one (undivided) he will be filled with light, yet whenever he is divided (chooses) he will be filled with darkness.

Luke 17:34 I tell you, on that night there will be two in one bed; one will be taken and the other left.

62. Jesus said: I tell my mysteries to those who are worthy of my mysteries. Do not let your right hand know what your left hand is doing.

Mark 4:11 And he said to them, To you has been given the secret of the kingdom of God, but for those outside, everything comes in parables.

Matthew 6:3 But when you give alms, do not let your left hand know what your right hand is doing.

Luke 8:10 He said, To you it has been given to know the secrets of the kingdom of God; but for others they are in parables, so that seeing they may not see, and hearing they may not understand.

Matthew 13:10 Then the disciples came and said to him, Why do you speak to them in parables? 11 And he answered them, To you it has been given to know the secrets of the kingdom of heaven, but to them it has not been given.

63. Jesus said: There was a wealthy person who had much money, and he said: I will use my money so that I may sow and reap and replant, to fill my storehouses with grain so that I lack nothing. This was his intention (is what he thought in his heart) but that same night he died. Whoever has ears, let him hear!

Luke 12:16 Then he told them a parable: The land of a rich man produced abundantly. 17 And he thought to himself, What should I do, for I have no place to store my crops? 18 Then he said, I will do this: I will pull down my barns and build larger ones, and there I will store all my grain and my goods. 19 And I will say to my soul, Soul, you have ample goods laid up for many years; relax, eat, drink, be merry. 20 But God said to him, You fool! This very night your life is being demanded of you. And the things you have prepared, whose will they be? 21 So it is with those who store up treasures for themselves but are not rich toward God.

64. Jesus said: A person had houseguests, and when he had prepared the banquet in their honor he sent his servant to invite the guests. He went to the first, he said to him: My master invites you. He replied: I have to do business with some merchants. They are coming to see me this evening. I will go to place my orders with them. I ask to be excused from the banquet. He went to another, he said to him: My master has invited you. He replied to him: I have just bought a house and they require me for a day. I will have no spare time. He came to another, he said to him: My master invites you. He replied to him: My friend is getting married and I must arrange a banquet for him. I will not be able to come. I ask to be excused from the banquet. He went to another, he said to him: My master invites you. He replied to him: I have bought a farm. I go to receive the rent. I will not be able to come. I ask to be excused. The servant returned, he said to his master: Those whom you have invited to the banquet have excused themselves. The master said to his servant: Go out to the roads, bring those whom you find so that they may feast. And he said: Businessmen and merchants will not enter the places of my Father.

Luke 14:16 Then Jesus said to him:, Someone gave a great dinner and invited many. 17 At the time for the dinner he sent his slave to say to those who had been invited, Come; for everything is ready now. 18 But they all alike began to make excuses. The first said to him, I have bought a piece of land, and I must go out and see it; please accept my regrets. 19 Another said, I have bought five yoke of oxen, and I am going to try them out; please accept my regrets. 20 Another said, I have just been married, and therefore I cannot come. 21 So the slave returned and reported this to his master. Then the owner of the house became angry and said to his slave, Go out at once into the streets and lanes of the town and bring in the poor, the crippled, the blind, and the lame. 22 And the slave said, Sir, what you ordered has been done, and there is still room. 23 Then the master said to the slave, Go out into the roads and lanes, and compel people to come in, so that my house may be filled. 24 For I tell you, none of those who were invited will taste my dinner.

Matthew 19:23 Then Jesus said to his disciples, Truly I tell you, it will be hard for a rich person to enter the kingdom of heaven.

Matthew 22:3 and sent his servants to call those who were invited to the marriage feast; but they would not come. 4 Again he sent other servants, saying, Tell those who are invited, Behold, I have made ready my dinner, my oxen and my fat calves are killed, and everything is ready; come to the marriage feast. 5 But they made light of it and went off, one to his farm, another to his business, 6 while the rest seized his servants, treated them shamefully, and killed them. 7 The king was angry, and he sent his troops and destroyed those murderers and burned their city. 8 Then he said to his servants, The wedding is ready, but those invited were not worthy. 9 Go therefore to the thoroughfares, and invite to the marriage feast as many as you find. 10 And those servants went out into the streets and gathered all whom they found, both bad and good; so the wedding hall was filled with guests. 11 But when the king came in to look at the guests, he saw there a man who had no wedding garment; 12 and he said to him, Friend, how did you get in here without a wedding garment? And he was speechless. 13 Then the king said to the attendants, Bind him hand and foot, and cast him into the outer darkness; there men will weep and gnash their teeth. 14 For many are called, but few are chosen.

65. He said: A kind person who owned a vineyard leased it to tenants so that they would work it and he would receive the fruit from them. He sent his servant so that the tenants would give to him the fruit of the vineyard. They seized his servant and beat him nearly to death. The servant went, he told his master what had happened. His master said: Perhaps they did not recognize him. So, he sent another servant. The tenants beat him also. Then the owner sent his son. He said: Perhaps they will respect my son. Since the tenants knew that he was the heir to the vineyard, they seized him and killed him. Whoever has ears, let him hear!

Matthew 21:33 Listen to another parable. There was a landowner who planted a vineyard, put a fence around it, dug a wine press in it, and built a watchtower. Then he leased it to tenants and went to another country. 34 When the harvest time had come, he sent his slaves to the tenants to collect his produce. 35 But the tenants seized his slaves and beat one, killed another, and stoned another. 36 Again he sent other slaves, more than the first; and they treated them in the same way. 37 Finally he sent his son to them, saying, They will respect my son. 38 But when the tenants saw the son, they said to themselves, This is the heir; come, let us kill him and get his inheritance. 39 So they seized him, threw him out of the vineyard, and killed him.

Mark 12:1 And he began to speak to them in parables. A man planted a vineyard, and set a hedge around it, and dug a pit for the wine press, and built a tower, and let it out to tenants, and went into another country. 2 When the time came, he sent a servant to the tenants, to get from them some of the fruit of the vineyard. 3 And they took him and beat him, and sent him away empty-handed. 4 Again he sent to them another servant, and they wounded him in the head, and treated him shamefully. 5 And he sent another, and him they killed; and so with many others, some they beat and some they killed. 6 He had still one other, a beloved son; finally he sent him to them, saying, They will respect my son. 7 But those tenants said to one another, This is the heir; come, let us kill him, and the inheritance will be ours. 8 And they took him and killed him, and cast him out of the vineyard. 9 What will the owner of the vineyard do? He will come and destroy the tenants, and give the vineyard to others.

Luke 20:9 And he began to tell the people this parable: A man planted a vineyard, and let it out to tenants, and went into another country for a long while. 10 When the time came, he sent a servant to the tenants, that they should give him some of the fruit of the vineyard; but the tenants beat him, and sent him away empty-handed. 11 And he sent another servant; him also they beat and treated shamefully, and sent him away empty-handed. 12 And he sent yet a third; this one they wounded and cast out. 13 Then the owner of the vineyard said, What shall I do? I will send my beloved son; it may be they will respect him. 14 But when the tenants saw him, they said to themselves, This is the heir; let us kill him, that the inheritance may be ours. 15 And they cast him out of the vineyard and killed him. What then will the owner of the vineyard do to them? 16 He will come and destroy those tenants, and give the vineyard to others. When they heard this, they said, God forbid!

66. Jesus said: Show me the stone which the builders have rejected. It is that one that is the cornerstone (keystone).

Matthew 21:42 Jesus said to them, Have you never read in the scriptures: The very stone which the builders rejected has become the head of the corner; this was the Lord's doing, and it is marvelous in our eyes?

Mark 12:10 Have you not read this scripture: The very stone which the builders rejected has become the head of the corner; 11 this was the Lord's doing, and it is marvelous in our eyes?

Luke 20:17 But he looked at them and said, What then does this text mean: The stone that the builders rejected has become the cornerstone?

67. Jesus said: Those who know everything but themselves, lack everything. (whoever knows the all and still feels a personal lacking, he is completely deficient).

68. Jesus said: Blessed are you when you are hated and persecuted, but they themselves will find no reason why you have been persecuted.

Matthew 5:11 Blessed are you when people revile you and persecute you and utter all kinds of evil against you falsely on my account.

Luke 6:22 Blessed are you when men hate you, and when they exclude you and revile you, and cast out your name as evil, on account of the Son of man!

69. Jesus said: Blessed are those who have been persecuted in their heart these are they who have come to know the Father in truth. Jesus said: Blessed are the hungry, for the stomach of him who desires to be filled will be filled.

Matthew 5:8 Blessed are the pure in heart, for they will see God.

Luke 6:21 Blessed are you who are hungry now, for you will be filled.

70. Jesus said: If you bring forth what is within you, it will save

you. If you do not have it within you to bring forth, that which you lack will destroy you.

71. Jesus said: I will destroy this house, and no one will be able to build it again.

Mark 14:58 We heard him say, I will destroy this temple that is made with hands, and in three days I will build another, not made with hands.

72. A person said to him: Tell my brothers to divide the possessions of my father with me. He said to him: Oh man, who made me a divider? He turned to his Disciples, he said to them: I'm not a divider, am I?

Luke 12:13 Someone in the crowd said to him, Teacher, tell my brother to divide the family inheritance with me. 14 But he said to him, Friend, who set me to be a judge or arbitrator over you? 15 And he said to them, Take care! Be on your guard against all kinds of greed; for one's life does not consist in the abundance of possessions.

73. Jesus said: The harvest is indeed plentiful, but the workers are few. Ask the Lord to send workers for the harvest.

Matthew 9:37 Then he said to his disciples, The harvest is plentiful, but the laborers are few; 38 therefore ask the Lord of the harvest to send out laborers into his harvest.

74. He said: Lord, there are many around the well, yet there is nothing in the well. How is it that many are around the well and no one goes into it?

75. Jesus said: There are many standing at the door, but only those who are alone are the ones who will enter into the Bridal Chamber.

Matthew 22:14 For many are called, but few are chosen.

76. Jesus said: The Kingdom of the Father is like a rich merchant who found a pearl. The merchant was prudent. He sold his fortune and bought the one pearl for himself. You also, seek for his treasure which does not fail, which endures where no moth can come near to eat it nor worm to devour it.

Matthew 13:45 Again, the kingdom of heaven is like a merchant in search of fine pearls; 46 on finding one pearl of great value, he went and sold all that he had and bought it.

Matthew 6:19 Do not store up for yourselves treasures on earth, where moth and rust consume and where thieves break in and steal; 20 but store up for yourselves treasures in heaven, where neither moth nor rust consumes and where thieves do not break in and steal.

77. Jesus said: "I-Am" the Light who is over all things, "I-Am" the All. From me all came forth and to me all return (The All came from me and the All has come to me). Split wood, there am I. Lift up the stone and there you will find me.

John 8:12 Again Jesus spoke to them, saying, I am the light of the world. Whoever follows me will never walk in darkness but will have the light of life.
John 1:3 All things came into being through him, and without him not one thing came into being.

78. Jesus said: Why did you come out to the wilderness; to see a reed shaken by the wind? And to see a person dressed in fine (soft – plush) garments like your rulers and your dignitaries? They are clothed in plush garments, and they are not able to

recognize (understand) the truth.

Matthew 11:7 As they went away, Jesus began to speak to the crowds about John: What did you go out into the wilderness to look at? A reed shaken by the wind? 8 What then did you go out to see? Someone dressed in soft robes? Look, those who wear soft robes are in royal palaces. 9 What then did you go out to see? A prophet? Yes, I tell you, and more than a prophet.

79. A woman from the multitude said to him: Blessed is the womb which bore you, and the breasts which nursed you! He said to her: Blessed are those who have heard the word (meaning) of the Father and have truly kept it. For there will be days when you will say: Blessed be the womb which has not conceived and the breasts which have not nursed.

Before the Gospels

Luke 11:27 While he was saying this, a woman in the crowd raised her voice and said to him, Blessed is the womb that bore you and the breasts that nursed you! 28 But he said, Blessed rather are those who hear the word of God and obey it!

Luke 23:29 For the days are surely coming when they will say, Blessed are the barren, and the wombs that never bore, and the breasts that never nursed.

80. Jesus said: Whoever has come to understand (recognize) the world (world system) has found a corpse, and whoever has found the corpse, of him the world (world system) is not worthy.

81. Jesus said: Whoever has become rich should reign, and let whoever has power renounce it.

82. Jesus said: Whoever is close to me is close to the fire, and whoever is far from me is far from the Kingdom.

83. Jesus said: Images are visible to man but the light which is within them is hidden. The light of the father will be revealed, but he (his image) is hidden in the light.

84. Jesus said: When you see your reflection, you rejoice. Yet when you perceive your images which have come into being before you, which neither die nor can be seen, how much will you have to bear?

85. Jesus said: Adam came into existence from a great power and a great wealth, and yet he was not worthy of you. For if he had been worthy, he would not have tasted death.

86. Jesus said: The foxes have their dens and the birds have their nests, yet the Son of Man has no place to lay his head for rest.

Matthew 8:20 And Jesus said to him, Foxes have holes, and birds of the air have nests; but the Son of Man has nowhere to lay his head.

87. Jesus said: Wretched is the body which depends upon another body, and wretched is the soul which depends on these two (upon their being together).

Before the Gospels

88. Jesus said: The angels and the prophets will come to you, and what they will give you what belongs to you. And you will give them what you have, and say among yourselves: When will they come to take (receive) what belongs to them?

89. Jesus said: Why do you wash the outside of your cup? Do you not understand (mind) that He who creates the inside is also He who creates the outside?

Luke 11:39 Then the Lord said to him, Now you Pharisees clean the outside of the cup and of the dish, but inside you are full of greed and wickedness. 40 You fools! Did not the one who made the outside make the inside also?

90. Jesus said: Come unto me, for my yoke is comfortable (natural) and my lordship is gentle— and you will find rest for yourselves.

Matthew 11:28 Come to me, all you that are weary and are carrying heavy burdens, and I will give you rest. 29 Take my yoke upon you, and learn from me; for I am gentle and humble in heart, and you will find rest for your souls. 30 For my yoke is easy, and my burden is light.

91. They said to him: Tell us who you are, so that we may believe

in you. He said to them: You examine the face of the sky and of the earth, yet you do not recognize Him who is here with you, and you do not know how to seek in (to inquire of Him at) this moment (you do not know how to take advantage of this opportunity).

John 9:36 He answered, And who is he, sir? Tell me, so that I may believe in him.

Luke 12:54 He also said to the crowds, When you see a cloud rising in the west, you immediately say, It is going to rain; and so it happens. 55 And when you see the south wind blowing, you say, There will be scorching heat; and it happens. 56 You hypocrites! You know how to interpret the appearance of earth and sky, but why do you not know how to interpret the present time?

Before the Gospels

92. Jesus said: Seek and you will find. But in the past I did not answer the questions you asked. Now I wish to tell them to you, but you do not ask about (no longer seek) them.

Matthew 7:7 Ask, and it will be given you; search, and you will find; knock, and the door will be opened for you.

93. Jesus said: Do not give what is sacred to the dogs, lest they throw it on the dung heap. Do not cast the pearls to the swine, lest they cause it to become dung (mud).

Matthew 7:6 Do not give what is holy to dogs; and do not throw your pearls before swine, or they will trample them under foot and turn and maul you.

94. Jesus said: Whoever seeks will find. And whoever knocks, it will be opened to him.

Matthew 7:8 For everyone who asks receives, and everyone who searches finds, and for everyone who knocks, the door will be opened.

95. Jesus said: If you have money, do not lend at interest, but rather give it to those from whom you will not be repaid.

Luke 6:34 If you lend to those from whom you hope to receive, what credit is that to you? Even sinners lend to sinners, to receive as much again. 35 But love your enemies, do good, and lend, expecting nothing in return. Your reward will be great, and you will be children of the Most High; for he is kind to the ungrateful and the wicked.

96. Jesus said: The Kingdom of the Father is like a woman who has taken a little yeast and hidden it in dough. She produced large loaves of it. Whoever has ears, let him hear!

Matthew 13:33 He told them another parable: The kingdom of heaven is like yeast that a woman took and mixed in with three measures of flour until all of it was leavened.

97. Jesus said: The Kingdom of the Father is like a woman who was carrying a jar full of grain. While she was walking on a road far from home, the handle of the jar broke and the grain poured out behind her onto the road. She did not know it. She had noticed no problem. When she arrived in her house, she set the jar down and found it empty.

98. Jesus said: The Kingdom of the Father is like someone who wished to slay a prominent person. While still in his own house

Before the Gospels

he drew his sword and thrust it into the wall in order to test whether his hand would be strong enough. Then he slew the prominent person.

99. His Disciples said to him: Your brethren and your mother are standing outside. He said to them: Those here who do my Father's desires are my Brethren and my Mother. It is they who will enter the Kingdom of my Father.

Matthew 12:46 While he was still speaking to the crowds, his mother and his brothers were standing outside, wanting to speak to him. 47 Someone told him, Look, your mother and your brothers are standing outside, wanting to speak to you. 48 But to the one who had told him this, Jesus replied, Who is my mother, and who are my brothers? 49 And pointing to his disciples, he said, Here are my mother and my brothers! 50 For whoever does the will of my Father in heaven is my brother and sister and mother.

100. They showed Jesus a gold coin, and said to him: The agents of Caesar extort taxes from us. He said to them: Give the things of Caesar to Caesar, give the things of God to God, and give to me what is mine.

Mark 12:14 Is it lawful to pay taxes to the emperor, or not? 15 Should we pay them, or should we not? But knowing their hypocrisy, he said to them,

Why are you putting me to the test? Bring me a denarius and let me see it. 16 And they brought one. Then he said to them, Whose head is this, and whose title? They answered, The emperor's. 12:17 Jesus said to them, Give to the emperor the things that are the emperor's, and to God the things that are God's. And they were utterly amazed at him.

101. Jesus said: Whoever does not hate his father and his mother as I do, will not be able to become my Disciple. And whoever does not love his Father and his Mother as I do, will not be able to become my Disciple. For my mother bore me, yet my true Mother gave me the life.

Matthew 10:37 Whoever loves father or mother more than me is not worthy of me; and whoever loves son or daughter more than me is not worthy of me.

102. Jesus said: Damn these Pharisees. They are like a dog sleeping in the feed trough of oxen. For neither does he eat, nor does he allow the oxen to eat.

Matthew 2:.13 But woe unto you, scribes and Pharisees, hypocrites! because you shut the kingdom of heaven against men; for you neither enter yourselves, nor allow those who would enter to go in.

103. Jesus said: Blessed is the person who knows at what place of the house the bandits may break in, so that he can rise and collect his things and prepare himself before they enter.

Matthew 24:43 But understand this: if the owner of the house had known in what part of the night the thief was coming, he would have stayed awake and would not have let his house be broken into.

104. They said to him: Come, let us pray today and let us fast. Jesus said: What sin have I committed? How have I been overcome (undone)? When the Bridegroom comes forth from the Bridal Chamber, then let them fast and let them pray.

105. Jesus said: Whoever acknowledges (comes to know) father and mother, will be called the son of a whore.

106. Jesus said: When you make the two one, you will become Sons of Man (children of Adam), and when you say to the mountain: Move! It will move.

Mark 11:23 Truly I tell you, if you say to this mountain, Be taken up and thrown into the sea, and if you do not doubt in your heart, but believe that what you say will come to pass, it will be done for you.

107. Jesus said: The Kingdom is like a shepherd who has a hundred sheep. The largest one of them went astray. He left the ninety-nine and sought for the one until he found it. Having searched until he was weary, he said to that sheep: I desire you more than the ninety-nine.

Matthew 18:12 What do you think? If a shepherd has a hundred sheep, and one of them has gone astray, does he not leave the ninety-nine on the mountains and go in search of the one that went astray? 13 And if he finds it, truly I tell you, he rejoices over it more than over the ninety-nine that never went astray.

108. Jesus said: Whoever drinks from my mouth will become like me. I will become him, and the secrets will be revealed to him.

109. Jesus said: The Kingdom is like a person who had a treasure hidden in his field and knew nothing of it. After he died, he bequeathed it to his son. The son accepted the field knowing nothing of the treasure. He sold it. Then the person who bought it came and plowed it. He found the treasure. He began to lend money at interest to whomever he wished.

Before the Gospels

Matthew 13:44 The kingdom of heaven is like treasure hidden in a field, which someone found and hid; then in his joy he goes and sells all that he has and buys that field.

110. Jesus said: Whoever has found the world (system) and becomes wealthy (enriched by it), let him renounce the world (system).

Mark 10:21 Then Jesus beholding him loved him, and said unto him, One thing thou lackest: go thy way, sell whatsoever thou hast, and give to the poor, and thou shalt have treasure in heaven: and come, take up the cross, and follow me. 22 And he was sad at that saying, and went away grieved: for he had great possessions. 23 And Jesus looked round about, and saith unto his disciples, How hardly shall they that have riches enter into the kingdom of God!

111. Jesus said: Heaven and earth will roll up before you, but he who lives within the Living-One will neither see nor fear death. For, Jesus said: Whoever finds himself, of him the world is not worthy.

112. Jesus said: Damned is the flesh which depends upon the soul. Damned is the soul which depends upon the flesh.

113. His Disciples said to him: When will the Kingdom come?

Jesus said: It will not come by expectation (because you watch or wait for it). They will not say: Look here! or: Look there! But the Kingdom of the Father is spread upon the earth, and people do not realize it.

Luke 17:20 And when he was demanded of by the Pharisees, when the kingdom of God should come, he answered them and said, The kingdom of God cometh not with observation: Neither shall they say, Lo-Here! Lo-There! For, behold, the kingdom of God is within you.

**(Saying 114 was written later and was added to the original text.)
114. Simon Peter said to them: Send Mary away from us, for women are not worthy of this life. Jesus said: Behold, I will draw her into me so that I make her male, in order that she herself will become a living spirit like you males. For every female who becomes male will enter the Kingdom of the Heavens.**

The Passion Narrative

According to tradition, Mark was not one of the original apostles, but rather a follower of one of them. Church historians tell us he followed Peter. One account places Mark in Rome, but another has him located at Alexandria. Since Mark supposedly wrote and translated for Peter, the story that we call Mark's gospel could have been derived from Peter. Whoever wrote the gospel attributed to Mark used several oral traditions, some of which had passed into written form, as components to construct the story. One of these sources is called the Passion Narrative.

Judging from its language and content, most scholars believe The Passion Narrative was written between 30 A.D. and 60 A.D. Mark used the document to construct the story of Jesus' trial, crucifixion, and burial. In Mark we can see the chronology behind the text.

There is lack of historical consistency between John and the other gospels. Because of the apparent discrepancy between the synoptic Gospels of Matthew, Mark and Luke and the Gospel of John one could argue there is evidence of differences in sources between John on one hand, and the synoptic gospels on the other. Since there are great differences it leaves one to hypothesize there could be at least two oral traditions containing the passion of Jesus. Either or both stories could have been preserved in written form and used by Mark, with his source and John with his separate source.

One such variance is the day Jesus died.

In the synoptic Gospels, Jesus offers the Lord's Supper "on the first day of unleavened bread, when they sacrificed the Passover lamb" (Mark 14:12; cf. Matt. 26:17, Luke 22:7). That would mean Jesus said the first Mass on Thursday, the fourteenth of Nisan. This was "the day of preparation" for the Passover when the lambs were slain and the meal prepared to be eaten in the evening according to Ex. 12:6. However, John tells us that Jesus was crucified on the "day of preparation" in John 19:31. That would seem to make Friday, the fourteenth of Nisan, the day of preparation. Saturday would then have been both the Sabbath and the Passover.

John's gospel is different in many respects from Matthew, Mark and Luke.

In John's gospel Jesus tells no parables, and speaks in a poetic style very different from his "voice" in the synoptic gospels. Another difference: in Matthew, Mark and Luke, the central moment of Jesus' "last supper" comes when he takes bread and wine and says "This is my body, this is my blood." This event isn't even mentioned in the gospel of John, which instead speaks of Jesus' washing his disciples' feet as the significant moment of this final meal.

In John's gospel, the "last supper" is described as a meal that takes place before the Passover (John 13:1). In John's gospel, Jesus dies on the cross on Passover. This enables John to make the theological and spiritual point that Jesus, the true "Lamb of God," dies at the exact hour the lambs that will be used for the Passover meals are being sacrificed in the Temple.

Although some have speculated that Jesus may have followed the Jewish sect called the Essenes, and they celebrated the Passover on a slightly different date, this would assume the authors jumped back and forth regarding dates without mentioning why or even mentioning the small sect at all. Even if it is true that all Jews in Jerusalem would not have been eating their Passover meal on exactly the same evening, it may not excuse the differences between the gospels.

The discrepancy in dating is perhaps best explained with the realization that the author of the gospel of John was using a different source in the writing of his gospel.

There is some evidence the source used by Mark, and carried over into Matthew, was Aramaic in origin.

When Jesus cries out to God, saying "My God, My God, why have you forsaken me, he uses the words "ELOI, ELOI, LAMA SABACHTHA or ELI, ELI, LAMA SABACHTHANI.

e'-loi, e-lo'i, la'-ma, sa-bakh-tha'-ni, or (Eloi, eloi, lama sabachthanei):

The forms of the first word as translated vary in the two narratives between Mark and Matthew.

The utterance is a variance of form probably from Psalms 22:1 ('eli 'eli lamah `azabhtani).

Psalm 22

New King James Version (NKJV)

The Suffering, Praise, and Posterity of the Messiah

To the Chief Musician. Set to "The Deer of the Dawn." A Psalm of David.

22 My God, My God, why have You forsaken Me?

Why are You so far from helping Me,

And from the words of My groaning?

O My God, I cry in the daytime, but You do not hear;

And in the night season, and am not silent.

The statement uttered by Jesus on the cross minutes before his death, just as from King David, is translated, "My God, my God, why hast thou forsaken me?" (Matthew 27:46; Mark 15:34). But there is a problem with this passage. There seems to be a mixture of Aramaic and Hebrew words.

The first two words, whether in Hebrew or Aramaic have different meanings to the crowd to warrant the jeer that Jesus was calling upon Elias, and not God. Mark gives the phrase and then explains to those who do not fully understand the language, that he was not calling on Elias, but on God.

According to Westcott and Hort's, *The New Testament in Greek*:

"The forms lema and lama used in Matthew and Mark respectively represent the various possible forms, the first in Aramaic, and the second in Hebrew.

The various readings and translations of the latter word, sabachthani, certainly has the influence of the Aramaic. Aramaic plays such a large part in the translation and transmission of the original meaning that it has led some to speculate that Mark's source for the passion of Jesus was likely in Aramaic. Mark would have written the phrase for the edification of the readers, not to confuse them."

There are other differences, between the synoptic gospels and John, which indicate not only a different source, but also a period of time the sources were written. One such point is the way Pilate is treated. Writers were well advised not to mention the names of powerful people in a negative context". By contrast, as shown by Philo and Josephus, Pilate "was the subject of more negative tradition than many other prefects and procurators," and so the creators of the original passion narrative had no reason not to mention Pilate by name and to place blame upon him. This situation is changed in the period after the First Jewish Revolt in the writings of Matthew and Luke, in which Pilate is exonerated and the high priest is named without hesitation.

On the naming of "James the younger," Theissen writes, "It would have been particularly necessary in Jerusalem to distinguish a 'James the younger' (or 'the less') from the 'older' (or 'greater') bearers of that name in the period circa 30-65 C.E."

Concerning the story of Barabbas, Theissen comments, "the text speaks quite simply of '*the* rebels,' who were taken prisoner during '*the* insurrection.' . . . We can only suppose that the text was composed before the next great uprising; after that, the author would have 'historicized' the account by distinguishing the previous 'stasis' from the more recent one. The next unrest with bloody clashes that struck Jerusalem was the appearance of Theudas under Cuspius Fadus (44-45 C.E.; cf. Acts 5:36, *Ant.* 20.97-98)."

Finally, there are two anonymous people in the story: the bystander who cuts off the ear of the high priest's slave with a sword (Mk 14:47) and a young man who escapes arrest by running away (Mk 14:51-52). Theissen writes (pp. 186-187):

"It seems to me that the narrative motive for this anonymity is not hard to guess: both of them run afoul of the "police." The one who draws his sword commits no minor offense when he cuts off someone's ear. Had the blow fallen only slightly awry, he could have wounded the man in the head or throat. This blow with a sword is violence with possibly mortal consequences. The anonymous young man has also offered resistance. In the struggle, his clothes are torn off, so that he has to run away naked. Both these people were in danger in the aftermath. As long as the high priest's slave was alive (and as long as the scar from the sword cut was visible) it would have been inopportune to mention their names; it would not even have been wise to identify them as members of the early Christian community. Their anonymity is for their protection, and the obscuring of their positive relationship to Jesus is a strategy of caution. Both the teller and the hearers know more about these two people. Only they could tell us who they were, whether Peter was the one with the sword, whether both are the same person, and whether reference was made to them in order to make the story of Jesus' end more credible."

Later, John would reveal it was Peter that cut the ear off the man, as we read in John 18:26-27. Being written around 130 A.D, enough time had passed there was no danger to Peter if the details were revealed or a name was added to the story.

Theissen writes: "If we are correct in our hypothesis of protective anonymity, the location of the Passion tradition would be unmistakable. Only in Jerusalem was there reason to draw a cloak of anonymity over followers of Jesus who had endangered themselves by their actions. The date could also be pinpointed: parts of the Passion account would have to have been composed within the generation of the eyewitnesses and their contemporaries, that is, somewhere between 30 and 60 C.E."

Although any one of these lines of evidence could be dismissed as coincidence, Theissen manages to create a series of plausible connections that make a case as a whole for the existence of an early pre-Markan passion narrative.

Before the Gospels

Where the passion story, or its source, ends is the final question. There are two theories. The first one is that it ended with the confession of the centurion. The second one is that the story ended with the appearance of Jesus to the disciples, which took place in Galilee.

By examining the language, word choices, structure, and flow of the Gospel of Mark, scholars have attempted to reconstruct the passion source.

Now, let us take a look at the Passion Narrative. The following depends on the Young's Literal Translation of the passion narrative in the Gospel of Mark, verses 14:32-15:47.

The Passion Narrative of Mark

Mark 14:32 And they come to a spot, the name of which [is] Gethsemane, and he saith to his disciples, `Sit ye here till I may pray;'

14:33 and he taketh Peter, and James, and John with him, and began to be amazed, and to be very heavy,

14:34 and he saith to them, `Exceeding sorrowful is my soul -- to death; remain here, and watch.'

14:35 And having gone forward a little, he fell upon the earth, and was praying, that, if it be possible the hour may pass from him,

14:36 and he said, `Abba, Father; all things are possible to Thee; make this cup pass from me; but, not what I will, but what Thou.'

14:37 And he cometh, and findeth them sleeping, and saith to Peter, `Simon, thou dost sleep! thou wast not able to watch one hour!

14:38 Watch ye and pray, that ye may not enter into temptation; the spirit indeed is forward, but the flesh weak.'

14:39 And again having gone away, he prayed, the same word saying;

Before the Gospels

14:40 and having returned, he found them again sleeping, for their eyes were heavy, and they had not known what they might answer him.

14:41 And he cometh the third time, and saith to them, `Sleep on henceforth, and rest -- it is over; the hour did come; lo, the Son of Man is delivered up to the hands of the sinful;

14:42 rise, we may go, lo, he who is delivering me up hath come nigh.'

14:43 And immediately -- while he is yet speaking -- cometh near Judas, one of the twelve, and with him a great multitude, with swords and sticks, from the chief priests, and the scribes, and the elders;

14:44 and he who is delivering him up had given a token to them, saying, `Whomsoever I shall kiss, he it is, lay hold on him, and lead him away safely,'

14:45 and having come, immediately, having gone near him, he saith, `Rabbi, Rabbi,' and kissed him.

14:46 And they laid on him their hands, and kept hold on him;

14:47 and a certain one of those standing by, having drawn the sword, struck the servant of the chief priest, and took off his ear.

14:48 And Jesus answering said to them, `As against a robber ye came out, with swords and sticks, to take me!

14:49 daily I was with you in the temple teaching, and ye did not lay hold on me -- but that the Writings may be fulfilled.'

14:50 And having left him they all fled;

14:51 and a certain young man was following him, having put a linen cloth about [his] naked body, and the young men lay hold on him,

14:52 and he, having left the linen cloth, did flee from them naked.

14:53 And they led away Jesus unto the chief priest, and come together to him do all the chief priests, and the elders, and the scribes;

14:54 and Peter afar off did follow him, to the inside of the hall of the chief priest, and he was sitting with the officers, and warming himself near the fire.

14:55 And the chief priests and all the sanhedrim were seeking against Jesus testimony -- to put him to death, and they were not finding,

14:56 for many were bearing false testimony against him, and their testimonies were not alike.

14:57 And certain having risen up, were bearing false testimony against him, saying --

14:58 `We heard him saying -- I will throw down this sanctuary made with hands, and by three days, another made without hands I will build;'

14:59 and neither so was their testimony alike.

14:60 And the chief priest, having risen up in the midst, questioned Jesus, saying, `Thou dost not answer anything! what do these testify against thee?'

14:61 and he was keeping silent, and did not answer anything. Again the chief priest was questioning him, and saith to him, `Art thou the Christ -- the Son of the Blessed?'

14:62 and Jesus said, `I am; and ye shall see the Son of Man sitting on the right hand of the power, and coming with the clouds, of the heaven.'

14:63 And the chief priest, having rent his garments, saith, `What need have we yet of witnesses?

14:64 Ye heard the evil speaking, what appeareth to you?' and they all condemned him to be worthy of death,

14:65 and certain began to spit on him, and to cover his face, and to buffet him, and to say to him, `Prophesy;' and the officers were striking him with their palms.

14:66 And Peter being in the hall beneath, there doth come one of the maids of the chief priest,

14:67 and having seen Peter warming himself, having looked on him, she said, `And thou wast with Jesus of Nazareth!'

14:68 and he denied, saying, `I have not known [him], neither do I understand what thou sayest;' and he went forth without to the porch, and a cock crew.

14:69 And the maid having seen him again, began to say to those standing near -- `This is of them;'

14:70 and he was again denying. And after a little again, those standing near said to Peter, `Truly thou art of them, for thou also art a Galilean, and thy speech is alike;'

14:71 and he began to anathematize, and to swear -- `I have not known this man of whom ye speak;'

14:72 and a second time a cock crew, and Peter remembered the saying that Jesus said to him -- `Before a cock crow twice, thou mayest deny me thrice;' and having thought thereon -- he was weeping.

15:1 And immediately, in the morning, the chief priests having made a consultation, with the elders, and scribes, and the whole sanhedrim, having bound Jesus, did lead away, and delivered [him] to Pilate;

15:2 and Pilate questioned him, `Art thou the king of the Jews?' and he answering said to him, `Thou dost say it.'

15:3 And the chief priests were accusing him of many things, [but he answered nothing.]

15:4 And Pilate again questioned him, saying, `Thou dost not answer anything! lo, how many things they do testify against thee!'

15:5 and Jesus did no more answer anything, so that Pilate wondered.

15:6 And at every feast he was releasing to them one prisoner, whomsoever they were asking;

15:7 and there was [one] named Barabbas, bound with those making insurrection with him, who had in the insurrection committed murder.

15:8 And the multitude having cried out, began to ask for themselves as he was always doing to them,

15:9 and Pilate answered them, saying, `Will ye [that] I shall release to you the king of the Jews?'

15:10 for he knew that because of envy the chief priests had delivered him up;

15:11 and the chief priests did move the multitude, that he might rather release Barabbas to them.

15:12 And Pilate answering, again said to them, `What, then, will ye [that] I shall do to him whom ye call king of the Jews?'

15:13 and they again cried out, `Crucify him.'

15:14 And Pilate said to them, `Why -- what evil did he?' and they cried out the more vehemently, `Crucify him;'

15:15 and Pilate, wishing to content the multitude, released to them Barabbas, and delivered up Jesus -- having scourged [him] -- that he might be crucified.

15:16 And the soldiers led him away into the hall, which is Praetorium, and call together the whole band,

15:17 and clothe him with purple, and having plaited a crown of thorns, they put [it] on him,

15:18 and began to salute him, `Hail, King of the Jews.'

15:19 And they were smiting him on the head with a reed, and were spitting on him, and having bent the knee, were bowing to him,

15:20 and when they [had] mocked him, they took the purple from off him, and clothed him in his own garments, and they led him forth, that they may crucify him.

15:21 And they impress a certain one passing by -- Simon, a Cyrenian, coming from the field, the father of Alexander and Rufus -- that he may bear his cross,

15:22 and they bring him to the place Golgotha, which is, being interpreted, `Place of a skull;'

15:23 and they were giving him to drink wine mingled with myrrh, and he did not receive.

15:24 And having crucified him, they were dividing his garments, casting a lot upon them, what each may take;

15:25 and it was the third hour, and they crucified him;

15:26 and the inscription of his accusation was written above -- `The King of the Jews.'

15:27 And with him they crucify two robbers, one on the right hand, and one on his left,

15:29 And those passing by were speaking evil of him, shaking their heads, and saying, `Ah, the thrower down of the sanctuary, and in three days the builder!

15:30 save thyself, and come down from the cross!'

15:31 And in like manner also the chief priests, mocking with one another, with the scribes, said, `Others he saved; himself he is not able to save.

Before the Gospels

15:32 The Christ! the king of Israel -- let him come down now from the cross, that we may see and believe;' and those crucified with him were reproaching him.

15:33 And the sixth hour having come, darkness came over the whole land till the ninth hour,

15:34 and at the ninth hour Jesus cried with a great voice, saying, `Eloi, Eloi, lamma sabachthani?' which is, being interpreted, `My God, my God, why didst Thou forsake me?'

15:35 And certain of those standing by, having heard, said, `Lo, Elijah he doth call;'

15:36 and one having run, and having filled a spunge with vinegar, having put [it] also on a reed, was giving him to drink, saying, `Let alone, let us see if Elijah doth come to take him down.'

15:37 And Jesus having uttered a loud cry, yielded the spirit,

15:38 and the veil of the sanctuary was rent in two, from top to bottom,

15:39 and the centurion who was standing over-against him, having seen that, having so cried out, he yielded the spirit, said, `Truly this man was Son of God.'

15:40 And there were also women afar off beholding, among whom was also Mary the Magdalene, and Mary of James the less, and of Joses, and Salome,

15:41 (who also, when he was in Galilee, were following him, and were ministering to him,) and many other women who came up with him to Jerusalem.

15:42 And now evening having come, seeing it was the preparation, that is, the fore-sabbath,

15:43 Joseph of Arimathea, an honourable counsellor, who also himself was waiting for the reign of God, came, boldly entered in unto Pilate, and asked the body of Jesus.

15:44 And Pilate wondered if he were already dead, and having called near the centurion, did question him if he were long dead,

15:45 and having known [it] from the centurion, he granted the body to Joseph.

15:46 And he, having brought fine linen, and having taken him down, wrapped him in the linen, and laid him in a sepulchre that had been hewn out of a rock, and he rolled a stone unto the door of the sepulchre,

Before the Gospels

15:47 and Mary the Magdalene, and Mary of Joses, were beholding where he is laid.

Mark

We have covered much regarding Mark, but let us recap briefly. The Gospel of Mark was written between 60 and 100 A.D. (with most scholars agreeing on 65 – 75 AD) by a person calling himself Mark, to whom Peter was recounting memories of his time with Jesus. Peter's memory, like most of ours, was freely running from one memory to another, as memories are chained together loosely and not in chronological order.

It also appears that Mark had access to the first parts of Q, or Q1 and maybe Q2, but not Q3. This leads us to wonder how much of Mark was built upon Peter's dictation and how much was taken from Q. It also appears that the Passion Narrative was used to set the times and order for the suffering and death of Jesus. Again, the question occurs of why the narrative was used and how much Peter remembered on his own. One could also ask the question suggesting that Peter or one of his acquaintances in the Jesus movement wrote part of Q and/or the Passion Narrative.

Justin Martyr spoke of Mark as being the memoirs of Peter (Dial. 106.3). In Acts 10:34-40, Peter's speech serves as a good summary of the Gospel of Mark, "beginning in Galilee after the baptism that John preached."

Before the Gospels

The NAB introduction to Mark says: "Petrine influence should not, however, be exaggerated. The evangelist has put together various oral and possibly written sources--miracle stories, parables, sayings, stories of controversies, and the passion--so as to speak of the crucified Messiah for Mark's own day."

John P. Meier states, "Prior to Mark's Gospel there seems to have been two cycles of traditions about Jesus' ministry in Galilee, each one beginning with one version of the feeding miracle (Mk 6:32-44 and Mk 8:1-10). Before these cycles were created, the two versions of the feeding would have circulated as independent units, the first version attracting to itself the story of Jesus' walking on the water (a development also witnessed in John 6), while the second version did not receive such an elaboration. Behind all three versions of the miracle story would have stood some primitive form."

Randel Helms writes concerning Mark 11:1 (Who Wrote the Gospels?, p. 6): "Anyone approaching Jerusalem from Jericho would come first to Bethany and then Bethphage, not the reverse. This is one of several passages showing that Mark knew little about Palestine; we must assume, Dennis Nineham argues, that 'Mark did not know the relative positions of these two villages on the Jericho road' (1963, 294-295). Indeed, Mark knew so little about the area that he described Jesus going from Tyrian territory 'by way of Sidon to the Sea of Galilee through the territory of the Ten Towns' (Mark 7:31). The simplist solution, says Nineham, is that 'the evangelist was not directly acquainted with Palestine'"

Although most place the date of Mark to be around 70 A.D. Others point to a single verse, which, if interpreted in a certain light would advance the date greatly. Verse 14 says: "When you see the 'Abomination of Desecration' standing where it should not be - let the reader take note! - those in Judea must flee to the mountains." The parenthetical comment to "let the reader take note" underscores the fact that this speech was written for the Christians of Mark's time. The contemporary audience of Mark would understand very well what he was talking about, although the 'Abomination of Desecration' is a cryptic reference to modern readers. The phrase is borrowed from Dn 9:27, where it refers to Antiochus profaning the Temple of Jerusalem c. 165 BC (probably with an image of Zeus), although it has been adapted to the evangelist's times. In the context of the First Jewish Revolt, this probably refers to the profanation of the Temple by the Romans. Josephus tells us that the victorious soldiers raised their imperial standards and worshiped them in the holy place (Wars of the Jews 6.6.1).

There is a significant modification to the end of Mark. Some time, just after it was penned and before many copies were made, through accident or mistreatment, the last page of one of the few copies of Mark was destroyed. New endings were added to several of the manuscripts as the damaged manuscript was copied. No less than four different endings have been found to the Gospel of Mark. It is thought the gospel ended simply, with the disciples going forth to teach and preach. The earliest manuscripts and some other ancient witnesses do not have verses 9–20.

Mark 16:9 When Jesus rose early on the first day of the week, he appeared first to Mary Magdalene, out of whom he had driven seven demons. 10 She went and told those who had been with him and who were mourning and weeping. 11 When they heard that Jesus was alive and that she had seen him, they did not believe it.
12 Afterward Jesus appeared in a different form to two of them while they were walking in the country. 13 These returned and reported it to the rest; but they did not believe them either.
14 Later Jesus appeared to the Eleven as they were eating; he rebuked them for their lack of faith and their stubborn refusal to believe those who had seen him after he had risen.
15 He said to them, "Go into all the world and preach the gospel to all creation. 16 Whoever believes and is baptized will be saved, but whoever does not believe will be condemned. 17 And these signs will accompany those who believe: In my name they will drive out demons; they will speak in new tongues; 18 they will pick up snakes with their hands; and when they drink deadly poison, it will not hurt them at all; they will place their hands on sick people, and they will get well."
19 After the Lord Jesus had spoken to them, he was taken up into heaven and he sat at the right hand of God. 20 Then the disciples went out and preached everywhere, and the Lord worked with them and confirmed his word by the signs that accompanied it.

Some manuscripts have the following ending between verses 8 and 9, and one manuscript has it after verse 8 (omitting verses 9-20): *Then they quickly reported all these instructions to those around Peter. After this, Jesus himself also sent out through them from east to west the sacred and imperishable proclamation of eternal salvation. Amen.*

The church settled on the ending of Mark we now use because it was powerful and it became the best known ending. The fact it did not appear in the original version may explain why every year the snake handling churches bury members who have died from snake bite and drinking poison.

Matthew

If Matthew used Mark as a source, the Gospel of Matthew must have been written after Mark. Scholars place the writing of Matthew between 80 and 100 A.D.

Matthew was written in Greek using Mark, Q, and the Septuagint as its sources. This is not what Eusebias tells us Papias said in his book. But then Eusebias tells us Papias was not very intelligent, and in Eusebias' opinion Papias was wrong in some of his assumptions, having misinterpreted information from various interviews of visitors to his area. No evidence has been found that points to Matthew being written in Hebrew, but it is not impossible that someone translated the book into Hebrew for their own use but it is more likely that the person referred to by Papias is not the Matthew we know.

Having first seen the construction of Mark, using the narrative Peter gave dictated to him, and part of the Q document to spur memory, we can now turn to Matthew and Luke, who used Mark as their foundation.

In 1951 B.H. Streeter set about to find how much of the Gospel of Mark was within the Gospel of Matthew. Taking a fresh approach to the language and structure he found that out of 666 verses in Mark, 600 of them occurred in Matthew. Hundreds of times the same words were used in the same order. Matthew is an expansion of Mark.

Herman N. Ridderbos writes (Matthew, p. 7):

This means, however, that we can no longer accept the traditional view of Matthew's authorship. At least two things forbid us to do so. First, the tradition maintains that Matthew authored an Aramaic writing, while the standpoint I have adopted does not allow us to regard our Greek text as a translation of an Aramaic original. Second, it is extremely doubtful that an eyewitness like the apostle Matthew would have made such extensive use of material as a comparison of the two Gospels indicates. Mark, after all, did not even belong to the circle of the apostles. Indeed Matthew's Gospel surpasses those of the other synoptic writers neither in vividness of presentation nor in detail, as we would expect in an eyewitness report, yet neither Mark nor Luke had been among those who had followed Jesus from the beginning of His public ministry.

J. C. Fenton argues (The Gospel of Saint Matthew, p. 12):

It is usually thought that Mark's Gospel was written about A.D. 65 and that the author of it was neither one of the apostles nor an eyewitness of the majority of the events recorded in his Gospel. Matthew was therefore dependent on the writing of such a man for the production of his book. What Matthew has done, in fact, is to produce a second and enlarged edition of Mark. Moreover, the changes which he makes in Mark's way of telling the story are not

Before the Gospels

those corrections which an eyewitness might make in the account of one who was not an eyewitness. Thus, whereas in Mark's Gospel we may be only one removed from eyewitnesses, in Matthew's Gospel we are at one removed further still.

Francis Write Beare notes (The Gospel according to Matthew, p. 7):

But the dependence of the book upon documentary sources is so great as to forbid us to look upon it as the work of any immediate disciple of Jesus. Apart from that, there are clear indications that it is a product of the second or third Christian generation. The traditional name of Matthew is retained in modern discussion only for convenience.

As for dating of the Gospel of Matthew, J.C. Fenton summarizes the evidence for the dating of Matthew as follows (op. cit., p. 11):

The earliest surviving writings which quote this Gospel are probably the letters of Ignatius, the Bishop of Antioch, who, while being taken as prisoner from the East to Rome about A.D. 110, wrote to various churches in Asia and Asia Minor and to the church at Rome. Ignatius refers to the star which appeared at the time of the birth of Jesus, the answer of Jesus to John the Baptist, when he was baptized, and several sayings of Jesus which are recorded only in this Gospel (12:33, 15:13, 19:12). It seems almost certain that Ignatius, and possibly the recipients of his letters also, knew this

Gospel, and thus that it was written before A.D. 110. But how long before?

Here we cannot be so certain. But it is possible that we can find evidence that Matthew was writing after the war between the Romans and the Jews which ended in the destruction of the temple at Jerusalem in A.D. 70. See, for example, 22:7: The king was angry, and he sent his troops and destroyed those murderers and burned their city; and compare also 21:41, 27:25. Similarly, Matthew's Gospel contains a strongly anti-Jewish note running through it, from the teaching not to do as the hypocrites do in Chapter 6, to the Woes on the scribes and Pharisees in Chapter 23; and this may point to a date after c. A.D. 85 when the Christians were excluded from the Jewish synagogues. It is worth noting here that Matthew often speaks of their synagogues (4:23, 9:35, 10:17, 12:9, 13:54), as if to distinguish Christian meetings and meeting places from those of the Jews, from which the Christians had now been turned out.

When a source is used the author will attempt to make the scenes, meanings, and information clearer and sharper to the reader. Ambiguities will be removed and meanings sharpened. One can see this in the scene of Jesus' baptism.

In Q (or the Sayings Gospel), as in Thomas, we see Jesus as a wise teacher. Mark reveals him as a "secret messiah." He is a teacher with divine guidance. In Matthew we see Jesus becoming divine.

Mark has the voice of God saying, "This is my beloved son. Listen to him."

Matthew writes the scene with the voice saying, "This is my beloved son on whom my favor rests."

Matthew attempts to make sure the readers understand this is God's messianic stamp of approval on Jesus.

In Mark we see Jesus in the tutelage of John the Baptist. In Matthew, John is simple there to announce Jesus' arrival and perform his baptism as a divine directive.

There are dozens of such re-interpretations, rewording, and embellishments between Mark and the other two synoptic gospels.

Luke

Most scholars place the dating of Luke between 80 and 130 A.D. The first element that stands out in Luke is that it is the men who do not believe in the resurrection of Jesus and it is the men who do not understand the significance. Although Luke follows Mark's account of the three women at the tomb, Luke tells us the women did not run and it was the women who reported it all to the men who did not believe them. Luke stresses the depth of wisdom and faith of the women. Luke even hints that the delay of the spirit at Pentecost may have been due to the fact that the men did not fully accept the resurrection. Further, passages, such as Luke 8:23 suggests there may have been more women than men in the crowd of believers.

These facts have led scholars, such as Randel McGraw Helms and others to speculate the writer of Luke may have been a woman.

From the outset, the author of Luke tells us that he or she was not an eyewitness, but was exposed to sources of information.

Luke 1:1 Forasmuch as many have taken in hand to set forth in order a declaration of those things which are most surely believed among us,

2 Even as they delivered them unto us, which from the beginning were eyewitnesses, and ministers of the word;

3 It seemed good to me also, having had perfect understanding of all things from the very first, to write unto thee in order, most excellent Theophilus,

4 That thou mightest know the certainty of those things, wherein thou hast been instructed.

These sources appear to be the Gospel of Mark and the Q document. Luke wrongly assumes, as we have also done, that Mark was an eyewitness. However, Mark wrote down what Peter told him about the events.

Luke was a native of the Hellenistic city of Antioch in Syria. Within scholarly circles, both secular and religious, there is lack of evidence as to the identity of the author of Luke. Luke is mentioned briefly a few times, and referred to as a doctor in the Pauline epistle to the Colossians. He is thought by most scholars to have been both a physician and a disciple of Paul. Luke was not an apostle but was probably a follower of Paul. This does not mean we should toss out the idea that Luke may have been a woman. After all, according to the book "The Acts of Paul and Thecla" (c.a.190A.D.) women were a large part of the Christian movement and there were no shortage of strong, intelligent, and wealthy women.

The author of Luke was very likely also the author of Acts. This has come to be so widely accepted that the two books are referred to as a single volume of Luke-Acts.

Edgar Goodspeed, in his book, The Work of Luke, tells us: "Luke and Acts are not two books, written at different times, but two volumes of a single work, conceived and executed as a unit. This distinction may not seem significant, but it is, as a matter of fact, of the utmost importance. It is one thing to write a pamphlet or a book;

it implies a certain degree of reflection, research, and organization. It is a very different thing to plan a book in two volumes, each in some degree a unit in itself but even more an integral part of a larger whole. Further, to recognize that Luke and Acts form two volumes of a single work enables us, so to speak, to gather all the light that each one of them has to throw on authorship, purpose, sources, date interest, etc., and focus it upon both of them."

Goodspeed goes on to say: " We have seen that the idea of writing such a work as Luke-Acts on the beginnings of the Christian movement could hardly have occurred to anyone until the Greek mission was a marked success and a great future had begun to open before the Christian faith. And wherever we test the book, it gives unmistakable signs of lateness of date, such as:

1. Its literary form is carefully organized into two volumes, each with its own distinct sphere and field and yet integrated with the other so as to be practically inseparable.

2. Its literary features are the preface, dedication, account of sources, purpose, and method.

3. Its infancy interest is pushed back to the birth of John. One is reminded that in the Book of James (the Protevangelium), half a century or more later, this infancy interest is pushed still farther back to the nativity of the Virgin herself.

4. Its resurrection interest include a whole series of appearances, visits, eatings, penetration of locked doors, protracted through forty days. This is in marked contrast to Matthew's (which was probably

also Mark's) account and is much nearer to the second-century representations of Jesus' long post-resurrection conversations with the apostles, e.g., the Epistle of the Apostles, ca. A.D. 150.

5. Its doctrine of the Holy Spirit pervades both volumes. The Holy Spirit is to come over Mary, 1:35; it fills Elizabeth, 1:42, and Zechariah, 1:67. It came down upon Jesus, 3:22; he was full of the Holy Spirit, 4:1. It is on almost every page of the Acts, the whole narrative of which seems to float upon a sea of it. Luke evidently has a definite and developed doctrine of the holy Spirit, which was the fruit of no little religious reflection.

6. The interest in punitive miracles is a feature conspicuous in the Elijah-Elisha cycles of Kings but wholly wanting from Mark and Matthew. It marks the opening scene of Luke (Zechariah is struck dumb) and plays a prominent part in the Acts: Ananias and Sapphira are struck dead, 5:5, 10; Elymas is struck blind, 13:11; compare 12:23. In this trait we are on our way to the fondness for punitive miracles in the infancy gospels of the second century, which also found it edifying, e.g., the Gospel of Thomas.

7. The passing of the Jewish controversy; this interest, so acute in Paul's day, has become a dead issue when Luke is written.

8. The interest in Christian psalmody. Luke preserves hymn after hymn, 1:42, 46, 68; 2:14, 29-the Magnificat, the Benedictus, the Gloria in Excelsis, the Nunc Dimittis. Nowhere else do we find any such early interest in Christian writings, except in Eph. 5:14 and in the arias, choruses, and antiphonies of the Revelation. Already that

liturgical endowment, which Walter Pater once said was one of the special gifts of the early church, was beginning to appear.

9. Church organization consists of the Twelve appear in the Acts as a sort of college of apostles, stationed in Jerusalem, watching over the progress of the Christian mission. With them are associated the elders, 15:2, 6, 22; 16:4, etc. Paul is represented as appointing elders in each church, 14:23, so the presbyteral organization is recognized as established, though Paul himself in his list of types of Christian leadership in I Cor. 12:28 says nothing about elders. The office of deacon is also traced back to the earliest days of the church and given added dignity and luster by the story of Stephen, chapters 6, 7. Luke's account of Ananias and Sapphira shows an interest in church funds when he wrote the Acts, and the story of Dorcas sewing for the poor, 9:39, also points to a considerable degree of organization. The point made here is not as to the fact of such embezzlement or charitable doings in the church, but of the writer's interest in recording them. Here belongs also the emphasis upon baptism as a condition of church membership, forgiveness, and salvation that is so characteristic of the Acts. 2:38; 8:12, 36; 9:18; 10:47; 16:15, 33.

10. The Speaking with Tongues was simply ecstatic utterance with Paul, I Corinthians, chapters 12-14, but in the Acts it has come to be a miraculous endowment with the power to speak foreign languages, Acts 2:4-11.

11. The circumstances of Paul's dead is that he is still living when the curtain falls upon the Acts in 28:30, 31, is outweighed by his

farewell to the Ephesian elders, 20:25, with its solemn declaration that none of them would ever see his face again, underscored by its repetition in 20:38: "they were especially saddened at his saying that they would never see his face again." Such presentiments are remembered and recorded only when they have proven true.

12. Paul has risen to hero stature. He is not only dead; he has become a hallowed memory. He is no longer a man struggling and grappling with difficulties, as in his letters; he has become a heroic figure and towers above priests, officers, governors, and kings. This is simply the retrospect of history. Lincoln rose in a generation into a heroic figure, very different from the man his contemporaries knew. The manner of his death no doubt contributed to this, but Paul's death too made its contribution to the reverence in which he came to be held, for he was probably the first of the Roman martyrs. Time has to play its part in the development of these attitudes. The success of the Greek mission naturally drew attention to the figure of the leader of that movement.

13. In the emergence of the sects, men of their own number were appearing and teaching perversions of the truth in order to draw the disciples away after them, 20:30. Apart from this reference to them in Acts the first we hear of the sects is in Eph. 4:14; compare 4:3-6, and in the Revelation, where the mysterious sect of the Nicolaitans is mentioned with abhorrence, 2:6, 15. Early in the second century the Docetists appear (cf. I, II John, Ignatius), then the Marcionites and Gnostics, and then the Montanists. Here, again. Acts seems to belong to the time of Ephesians and the Revelation.

14. Nonacquaintance with Paul's collected letters. The letters of Paul would have been of great value to the writer of the Acts; if he had known them, he could not have helped making use of them along with the numerous sources he mentions in his preface. It is next to impossible, if one knows Paul's letters, not to reveal the fact when writing about his life and work. They are ideal materials for such a task. But the Acts nowhere betrays any knowledge of them.

15. The situation presupposed by the conception of such a work-the wide success achieved by the Greek mission.

Luke-Acts might be still more definitely dated if it could be shown that Luke made use in it of the Antiquities of Josephus, which appeared in A.D. 93. The chief points of resemblance are the Theudas-Judas passage, Ant. xx. 5. 1, 2 (cf. Acts 5:36, 37), and the Lysanias reference, Ant. xx. 7. 1 (cf. Luke 3:1, 2), but, in both, matters are so very differently understood and stated in the Acts that it seems more probable that the two accounts are not immediately related to each other. If Luke used Josephus, he put Judas in the time of Quirinius' census after the Theudas of the times of Fadus, forty years later, and represented Lysanias as still tetrarch of Abilene sixty-five years after his death. Even the best of modern critical writers do not always escape just such errors, but it would be strange for Luke to do this if he really had Josephus.

It is not too much to say that, wherever we sound the book of Acts, the result is the same; it reveals itself as a work of the last decade of the first century. Even two or three of the considerations just listed would make such a date highly probable, but taken altogether they are overwhelming. Such points are too often dismissed as "difficulties" or dealt with atomistically-one at a time-the others being momentarily put aside. But it is their cumulative effect that is so significant. They are, as a matter of fact, clues to the solution of the problem of the date of the two volumes, and they may fairly be said to demonstrate that Acts (and Luke of course with it), was written about A.D. 90, about the time of Ephesians and Revelation but probably before the regulations of Domitian had brought the church acutely into collision with the empire over the matter of emperor worship." (This ends the quote from Goodspeed.)

Thus, we know with some certainty that the Gospel of Luke was written after 93 A.D. since Luke, whoever he or she may be, used the works of Josephus and Luke refers to emperor worship as a point of contention with Rome and the cause of execution of many Christians.

Tradition has Luke dying in Greece around 74 A.D. The conclusion hardly needs pointing out that the dates set here exclude Luke from being the author of the Gospel bearing his or her name.

Thus far we have Mark, who was not an eyewitness, but was writing down what Peter remembered, although his memory did not allow things to be written in chronological order. We believe Mark has access to the first two layers of Q but not the complete document. We have Luke admitting from the start he or she was not an eyewitness but was combining sources. And we have Matthew, who obviously used Mark's Gospel and Q, along with their personal additions, to write his gospel.

Joseph Lumpkin

The further back we go the more important Q becomes.

John

The Gospel of John, of course, stands apart from the other gospels because Matthew and Luke use common sources. They both use the gospel of Mark. They both use the so-called Q, or the synoptic sayings gospel. Similarities are evident, particularly the outline of the ministry of Jesus. The Gospel of John uses another source, called Signs Source. John also has some relationships to the sources used by the other gospels. He seems to use the same passion narrative as in Mark, Matthew, Luke and in the Gospel of Peter. The other thing that is common with the other gospels is a chain of miracle stories.

The major speeches in the gospel of John are developed out of traditional sayings materials but many of the sayings or monologs John records have parallels in the Gospel of Thomas. So John draws on a different set of traditional sayings of Jesus than do the first three gospels of the New Testament.

The personality and teachings of Jesus are quite different in John. Here, Jesus is in hostile opposition to the established Jewish leaders. It is likely the Christian faith was developing its own identity and breaking away from mainline Jewish worship, and thus being persecuted for it.

In John, Jesus explains who and what he is, revealing his theological place more than in the other Gospels. This developed theological reflection grows out of a different circle and tradition. The world was a Greek world with Greek sensibilities and Greek philosophies. Matthew, Mark , and Luke were plain, unadorned gospels. Their opening statements would have left Greek readers yawning, but John begins like a Greek would have written it. Indications are that the church was beginning to put together its complex doctrine, which would be influenced by the soaring Greek thoughts and pros.

John seems thoroughly Greek in character . Its thought and its literary and dialogue styles are thoroughly Greek. It has comparatively limited use of the Jewish scriptures (roughly about one-fifth of Matthew's). Its definite purpose, to strip Christianity of its Jewishness and give it a Greek face. This is also backed up by its anti-Jewish feeling, and its great debt to the mystery. Greeks loved a good mystery religion. Indications are the writer was a Greek, not a Jew.

Alfred Loisy, in his work, "The Origins of the New Testament" states: "The first publication can hardly have been effected before 135-140 (A.D.); the additions and retouches on synoptic lines will have been introduced soon afterwards when Asiatic Christianity was uniting with that of other churches to make common front against the flood of gnosticism and especially against Marcion. It is none the less true that the fourth Gospel is, essentially, a gnostic document, although its structure-form proclaims it a Christian catechism: moreover it has absorbed a number of gnostic pieces, rhythmic utterances of mystic teaching, originally composed outside the Gospel framework and incorporated with it by methods to be indicated presently, just as the Synoptics have incorporated many a fragment of the earlier eschatological teaching. The result is that the Johannine catechesis is hardly less complex than the synoptic."

Loisy continues, "Towards the end of the first century or the beginning of the second there lived a mystic prophet, a master of gnosis rather than an apostle of the faith, from whom came forth the hymns and symbolic visions on which the fourth Gospel is founded. A little later, towards 135-140, his sublime meditations were collected and framed in a Gospel story, to be used as a manual of initiation into the Christian faith, like other books of similar form already in circulation among the churches. The chronological framework was probably fixed at the same time and a part of the borrowings made from the synoptic tradition. At this stage and in this form the book had no author's name attached to it and its diffusion was limited, or nearly so, to the province of Asia. Some fifteen or twenty years later, towards 150-160, the Marcionite heresy having broken out, this Asiatic book was amended, completed and more or less worked over, not only by the addition of chapter xxi, but by other retouches and additions in the main body; it was then boldly presented as the work of an apostle. But everything was welcome that gave satisfaction to faith, and the result just described was accepted by those whose will-to-believe found the truth in it. Thus it came to pass that, when the Montanist controversy broke out, the adversaries of these pretended writings of the apostle John found nobody to listen to them. When later, towards 190, the great controversy arose about the keeping of Easter, the Roman Church failed to perceive, or pretended not to perceive that, while the

Synoptics supported the ritual tradition of Rome and of most other Christian churches, the fourth Gospel supported the different tradition followed by the churches of Asia." (This ends the quotes from Loisy.)

It is widely accepted that the source material of John is different from the synoptic gospels. Scholars believe he used something called the Signs Gospel. Let us look at the hypothetical source as scholars have used linguistics and comparisons of writing styles to pull from John's Gospel his source.

The Signs Gospel

The Signs Gospel is a hypothetical document, which recorded the life of Jesus. Some scholars believe it to be a primary source document used by John as the foundational information for the writing of the Gospel of John. As with the hypothesis of the Q and Passion sources, this theory has its basis in source criticism. In 1941 the scholar, Rudolf Bultmann, put forth a theory called the Hypothesis of a Semeia (signs or miracles) Source. The idea has gained wide acceptance.

Just as Q was written in layers over time and Mark depended on Q as his foundational information, Bultmann's hypothesis holds that the Gospel of John was composed in layers over a period of time with the author (or authors) of John building upon the previous work of the Signs author, who wrote an earlier, and likely more lean account of the life and miracles of Jesus.

The "Signs Gospel" was independent of, and not used by, the authors of the synoptic gospels, which is why the Gospel of John is so different in content and tone from Matthew, Mark, and Luke.

It is believed the Signs Gospel was circulating before the year 70 A.D. and was probably written between 50 and 70 A.D. The fact that John may not have been the final author of the Gospel of John does not mean he was not a contributor to the Gospel. The Gospel of John is dated between 90 and 120 A.D. and thus not likely written by the disciple. Raymond Edward Brown believed that the original author of the Signs Gospel to be John the Beloved Disciple.

D. Moody Smith comments (*Johannine Christianity*, p. 63): "It is now rather widely agreed that the Fourth Evangelist drew upon a miracle tradition or written source(s) substantially independent of the synoptics, whether or not he had any knowledge of one or more of those gospels. Since the epoch-making commentary of Rudolf Bultmann, the hypothesis of a *semeia-* (or miracle) source has gained rather wide acceptance."

Norman Perrin writes (*The New Testament: An Introduction*, p. 225): "But there is one source whose use must be recognized: a signs source.
In 2:11 Jesus' miracle at Cana is described as "the first of his signs." Further signs are mentioned in general terms in 2:23, and in 4:54 the

healing of the official's son at Capernaum is described as "the second sign that Jesus did when he had come from Judea to Galilee." Then 12:37 says, "Though he had done so many signs before them, yet they did not believe in him," and this note is sounded again in the closing summary of the gospel proper, 20:30-31: "Now Jesus did many other signs in the presence of the disciples, which are not written in this book; but these are written that you may believe. . . ." The possibility that in his narrative up to 12:37 the evangelist had used a source other than the synoptic gospels or the tradition represented by those gospels is strengthened since all the other miracles in John that are not paralleled in the synoptic gospels occur before 12:37: the healing at the pool of Bethzatha (5:1-9); the healing of the blind man (9:1-12); the raising of Lazarus (11:1-44). These miracles are generally on a grander and more elaborate scale than those in the synoptic gospels and seem to go further in presenting Jesus as a Hellenistic "divine man." Throughout the gospel until 12:37-38, and again in 20:30-31, the miracles are presented as intending to call forth faith: 2:11; 4:53; 6:14; 7:31; 11:45, 47b-48; 12:37-38; 20:31. Whereas in the synoptic gospels the emphasis is on faith as the prerequisite for miracles (e.g., Mark 6:5-6), here in the gospel of John miracles induce faith. These references not only contrast with the synoptic gospels, they also contrast with the remainder of the gospel of John itself. In 2:23-25 as in 4:48, Jesus repudiates the kind of faith induced by signs. The conversation with Nicodemus contrasts such faith unfavorably with rebirth "from above" and "of the spirit" (3:2, 3, 5-6). These factors make it very probable that the author of the gospel of John is using as a source and *reinterpreting* a book of signs that presents Jesus as a Hellenistic "divine man" whose miracles induce faith."

Kysar writes (*The Anchor Bible Dictionary*, v. 3, pp. 921-922): "The most widely held proposal for a literary source is that of a *signs source*. A number of things in the gospel contribute to the effort to reconstruct such a source: The presence of the series of wonder stories in the narrative, the unique use of the word, *semeia* ("signs"), to designate such wonders, the numbering of the signs in 2:11 and 4:54, and the reference to signs in the conclusion of the gospel. ...What is proposed is that there was a collection of the wonders of Jesus circulating within the Johannine community prior to the writing of the gospel. Efforts to reconstruct such a signs source from the gospel vary. At one extreme is the argument that it contained not only the wonders narrated in the gospel, but also the calling of the disciples in 1:19-51 and a passion story. At the other extreme is the suggestion that the collection was little more than seven wonder stories told consecutively. Some such theory is embraced by a large number of Johannine scholars, but by no means has agreement been reached on such a proposal."

Fortna states (op. cit., p. 19): "The following deeds of Jesus, less the Johannine insertions they now contain, would have comprised the bulk of SQ: changing water into wine (2:1-11), healing an official's son (4:46-54) and a lame man (5:2-9), feeding the multitude (6:1-14) - probably together with crossing the sea (6:15-25), giving sight to a blind man (9:1-8), and raising Lazarus (11:1-45). (Some would also include the catch of fish now found at 21:1-14.) An articulated series emerges from the reconstruction, not merely a gather of miracle stories, and a few other passages are also to be included: part of chap. 1 (at least the gathering of the first disciples in vv 35-49) as introduction and, as conclusion, 20:30-31a, and perhaps also parts of 12:37-41."

Did the Signs Gospel contain only miracles or was it a book recounting the teachings of Jesus also? Did it include his discourses and sermons, or was the author simply reporting miracles in order to evoke faith and wonder in the reader? The Signs Gospel (or SQ as some have designated it) is used to transmit to us that feeling seen in the stories when those who were exposed to his miracles and wonders knew immediately by their power that the man performing them was indeed the one so long anticipated. The messiah.

After concluding there is a high probability that the Signs Gospel exists, and is embedded within the Gospel of John, the most difficult task remaining is the parsing of the Gospel of John to expose the Signs Gospel within it. This is done by using clues within the Gospel of John, such as phrases indicating "this is the first sign (miracle or wonder)" and other such interesting hints that may lead to the conclusion the information was pulled from a source containing a list of stories. Another clue is a shift on wording, voice, tone, and even cadence of speech, which would occur as the Gospel of John shifts from one writer to another.

We will rely on Robert Fortuna's work for this parsing. A copy of this is found in Andrew Bernhard's book, The Lost Gospels. In Bernhard's book he states, "The following reconstruction of the hypothetical source employed by the author of the fourth gospel is derived from the analysis found in Robert Fortna's The Fourth Gospel and Its Predecessor. The text of the Signs Gospel has been reconstructed using the New Revised Standard Version (NRSV) of the Gospel of John; differences between the text of the Signs Gospel and the NRSV are printed in italics."

Verses are in the order in which they were thought to occur in the original Signs Gospel.

The Signs Gospel

John 1

(6) There was a man sent from God, whose name was John. (7) He came as a witness, so that all might believe through him.
(19) This is the testimony given by John when priests and Levites *came* to ask him, "Who are you?"
(20) *He* confessed, "I am not the Messiah."
(21) And they asked him, "What then? Are you Elijah?"
He said, "I am not."
"Are you the prophet?"
He answered, "No."
(22) Then they said to him, "Who are you? What do you say about yourself?"
(23) He said, "I am the voice of one crying out in the wilderness, 'Make straight the way of the Lord,' " as the prophet Isaiah said. I baptize with water. Among you stands (27) the one who is coming after me; I am not worthy to untie the thong of

his sandal."

(28) He saw Jesus coming toward him and declared, "Here is the Lamb of God. I came for this reason, that he might be revealed to Israel. I saw the Spirit descending from heaven like a dove on him. (34) And I myself have seen and have testified that this is the Son of God."

(35) *Now* John was standing with two of his disciples *who* heard him say this, and they followed Jesus. (38) They said to him, "Rabbi, where are you staying?" (39) He said to them, "Come and see." They came and saw where he was staying, and they remained with him that day. It was about four o'clock in the afternoon.

(40) One of the two who heard John speak and followed him was Andrew. (41) He first found his brother Simon and said to him, "We have found the Messiah." (42) He brought Simon to Jesus, who looked at him and said, "You are Simon son of John. You are to be called Cephas."

He found Philip and *Jesus* said to him,

"Follow me." (44) Now Philip was from Bethsaida, the city of Andrew and Peter. (45) Philip found Nathanael and said to him, "We have found him about whom Moses in the law wrote, Jesus son of Joseph from Nazareth."
(46) Nathanael said to him, "Can anything good come out of Nazareth?"
Philip said to him, "Come and see."
(47) When Jesus saw Nathanael coming toward him, he said of him, "Here is truly an Israelite."
(49) Nathanael replied, "Rabbi, you are the Son of God! You are the King of Israel!"

John 2

(1) There was a wedding in Cana, and the mother of Jesus was there. (2) Jesus and his disciples had also been invited to the wedding. (3) When the wine gave out, the mother of Jesus said to the servants, "Do whatever he tells you." (6) Now standing there were six stone water jars, each holding twenty or thirty gallons.
(7) Jesus said to them, "Fill the jars with

water." And they filled them up to the brim.

(8) He said to them, "Now draw some out, and take it to the chief steward." So they took it.

(9) When the steward tasted the water that had become wine, the steward called the bridegroom (10) and said to him, "Everyone serves the good wine first, and then the inferior wine after the guests have become drunk. But you have kept the good wine until now."

(11) Jesus did this, the first of his signs; and his disciples believed in him.

(12) After this he went down to Capernaum with his disciples.

John 4

(46) Now there was a royal official whose son lay ill in Capernaum. (47) He went and said to him, "Sir, come down before my little boy dies."

(50) Jesus said, "Go; your son will live." The man started on his way. (51) As he was going down, his slaves met him and told him that his child was alive. (52) So he asked them the hour when he began to recover, and they said to him, "Yesterday

at one in the afternoon the fever left him." (53) So he himself believed, along with his whole household.
(54) Now this was the second sign that Jesus did.

John 21

(2) Gathered there together were Simon Peter, Thomas called the Twin, Nathanael of Cana, the sons of Zebedee. (3) Simon Peter said to them, "I am going fishing." They said to him, "We will go with you." They went out and got into the boat, but that night they caught nothing.
(4) Just after daybreak, Jesus stood on the beach. (6) He said to them, "Cast the net to the right side of the boat, and you will find some."
So they cast it, and now they were not able to haul it in because there were so many fish. (7) Simon Peter put on some clothes and jumped into the sea (8) for they were not far from the land, only about a hundred yards off. (11) So Simon Peter went *ashore* and hauled the net ashore, full of large fish, a hundred fifty-three of them; and though there were so

many, the net was not torn. (14) This was now the third *sign* that Jesus *did before* the disciples.

John 6

(1) After this Jesus went to the other side of the Sea of Tiberias. (3) *He* went up the mountain and sat down there with his disciples. (5) When he looked up and saw a large crowd coming toward him, Jesus said to Philip, "Where are we to buy bread for these people to eat?"
(7) Philip answered him, "Six months' wages would not buy enough bread for each of them to get a little."
(8) One of his disciples said to him, (9) "There is a boy here who has five barley loaves and two fish. But what are they among so many people?"
(10) Jesus said, "Make the people sit down." Now there was a great deal of grass in the place; so they sat down, about five thousand in all. (11) Then Jesus took the loaves, and when he had given thanks, he distributed them to those who were seated; so also the fish, as much as they wanted.

Before the Gospels

(13) And from the fragments of the five barley loaves, left by those who had eaten, they filled twelve baskets. (14) When the people saw the sign that he had done, they began to say, "This is indeed the prophet who is to come into the world."
(15) *Jesus* withdrew again to the mountain by himself. (16) When evening came, his disciples went down to the sea, (17) got into a boat, and started across the sea to Capernaum. (18) The sea became rough because a strong wind was blowing. (19) When they had rowed about three or four miles, they saw Jesus walking on the sea, and they were terrified. (20) But he said to them, "It is I; do not be afraid." (21) And immediately the boat reached the land toward which they were going.

John 11

(1) Now a certain Mary; (2) her brother Lazarus was ill. (3) *She* sent a message to Jesus, "Lord, he whom you love is ill."
(7) He said to the disciples, "Our friend Lazarus has fallen asleep. Let us go to him."

(17) When Jesus arrived, he found that Lazarus had already been in the tomb four days. (32) When Mary saw him, she knelt at his feet and said to him, "Lord, if you had been here, my brother would not have died."

(33) When Jesus saw her weeping, he was greatly disturbed in spirit and deeply moved. (34) He said, "Where have you laid him?"

They said to him, "Lord, come and see."

(38) Then Jesus came to the tomb. It was a cave, and a stone was lying against it. (39) Jesus said, "Take away the stone." *Then* he cried with a loud voice, "Lazarus, come out!"

(44) The dead man came out, his hands and feet bound with strips of cloth, and his face wrapped in a cloth. Jesus said to them, "Unbind him, and let him go."

(45) *Those who* had seen what Jesus did, believed in him.

John 9

(1) As he walked along, he saw a man blind from birth. (6) He spat on the ground and made mud with the saliva

and spread the mud on the man's eyes, (7) saying to him, "Go, wash in the pool of Siloam." Then he went and washed and came back able to see. (8) The neighbors and those who had seen him before as a beggar began to ask, "Is this not the man who used to sit and beg?"

John 5

(2) Now in Jerusalem by the Sheep Gate there is a pool, called in Hebrew Beth-zatha, which has five porticoes. (3) In these lay many invalids—blind, lame, and paralyzed. (5) One man was there who had been ill for thirty-eight years. (6) When Jesus saw him lying there and knew that he had been there a long time, he said to him, "Do you want to be made well?"
(7) The sick man answered him, "Sir, I have no one to put me into the pool when the water is stirred up; and while I am making my way, someone else steps down ahead of me."
(8) Jesus said to him, "Stand up, take your mat and walk."
(9) At once the man was made well, and

he took up his mat and began to walk.

John 2

(14) In the temple *Jesus* found people selling cattle, sheep, and doves, and the money changers seated at their tables. (15) Making a whip of cords, he drove all of them out of the temple, both the sheep and the cattle. He also poured out the coins of the money changers and overturned their tables. (16) He told those who were selling the doves, "Take these things out of here! Stop making my Father's house a marketplace!"
(18) The Jews then said to him, "What sign can you show us for doing this?"
19 Jesus answered them, "Destroy this temple, and in three days I will raise it up."

John 11

(47) So the chief priests called a meeting of the council, and said, "This man is performing many signs. (48) If we let him go on like this, everyone will believe in him, and the Romans will come and

destroy our nation." (49) But one of them, Caiaphas, who was high priest that year, said to them, (50) "It is better for you to have one man die for the people than to have the whole nation destroyed." (53) So from that day on they planned to put him to death.

John 12

(37) Although he had performed so many signs, they did not believe in him. (38) This was to fulfill the word spoken by the prophet Isaiah: "Lord, who has believed our message, and to whom has the arm of the Lord been revealed?" (39) And so they could not believe, because Isaiah also said, (40) "He has blinded their eyes and hardened their heart, so that they might not look with their eyes, and understand with their heart and turn— and I would heal them."

(1) Six days before the Passover Jesus came to Bethany, the home of Lazarus, whom he had raised from the dead. (2) There they gave a dinner for him. Martha served, and Lazarus was one of those at the table with him. (3) Mary took a pound

of costly perfume made of pure nard, anointed Jesus, and wiped them with her hair. The house was filled with the fragrance of the perfume.

(4) But Judas Iscariot, one of his disciples, said, (5) "Why was this perfume not sold for three hundred denarii and the money given to the poor?"

(7) Jesus said, "She bought it so that she might keep it for the day of my burial. (8) You always have the poor with you, but you do not always have me."

(12) The next day the great crowd that had come to the festival heard that Jesus was coming to Jerusalem. (13) So they took branches of palm trees and went out to meet him, shouting, "Hosanna! Blessed is the one who comes in the name of the Lord— the King of Israel!"

(14) Jesus found a young donkey and sat on it; as it is written: (15) "Do not be afraid, daughter of Zion. Look, your king is coming, sitting on a donkey's colt!"

Before the Gospels

John 13   (1) Now before the festival of the Passover, Jesus knew that his hour had come to depart from this world and go to the Father. Having loved his own who were in the world, he loved them to the end. (2) The devil had already put it into the heart of Judas son of Simon Iscariot to betray him. And during supper (3) Jesus, knowing that the Father had given all things into his hands, and that he had come from God and was going to God, (4) got up from the table, took off his outer robe, and tied a towel around himself. (5) Then he poured water into a basin and began to wash the disciples' feet and to wipe them with the towel that was tied around him. (6) He came to Simon Peter, who said to him, "Lord, are you going to wash my feet?"
(7) Jesus answered, "You do not know now what I am doing, but later you will understand."
(8) Peter said to him, "You will never wash my feet."
Jesus answered, "Unless I wash you, you have no share with me."
(9) Simon Peter said to him, "Lord, not my

feet only but also my hands and my head!"

(10) Jesus said to him, "One who has bathed does not need to wash, except for the feet, but is entirely clean. And you are clean, though not all of you." (11) For he knew who was to betray him; for this reason he said, "Not all of you are clean." (12) After he had washed their feet, had put on his robe, and had returned to the table, he said to them, "Do you know what I have done to you? (13) You call me Teacher and Lord—and you are right, for that is what I am. (14) So if I, your Lord and Teacher, have washed your feet, you also ought to wash one another's feet. (15) For I have set you an example, that you also should do as I have done to you. (16) Very truly, I tell you, servants are not greater than their master, nor are messengers greater than the one who sent them. (17) If you know these things, you are blessed if you do them. (18) I am not speaking of all of you; I know whom I have chosen. But it is to fulfill the scripture, 'The one who ate my bread has lifted his heel against me.' (19) I tell you

this now, before it occurs, so that when it does occur, you may believe that I am he. (20) Very truly, I tell you, whoever receives one whom I send receives me; and whoever receives me receives him who sent me."

John 18

(1) Jesus went out with his disciples across the Kidron valley to a place where there was a garden. (2) Now Judas, who betrayed him, also knew the place, because Jesus often met there with his disciples. (3) So Judas brought a detachment of soldiers together with police from the chief priests, and they came there with lanterns and torches and weapons. (4) Then Jesus asked them, "Whom are you looking for?"
(5) They answered, "Jesus of Nazareth." Jesus replied, "I am he."
(10) Then Simon Peter, who had a sword, drew it, struck the high priest's slave, and cut off his right ear. The slave's name was Malchus.
(11) Jesus said to Peter, "Put your sword back into its sheath. Am I not to drink the

cup that the Father has given me?" (12) So the soldiers, their officer, and the Jewish police arrested Jesus and bound him.

(13) First they took him to Annas, who was the father-in-law of Caiaphas, the high priest that year. (15) Simon Peter and another disciple followed Jesus. Since that disciple was known to the high priest, he went with Jesus into the courtyard of the high priest, (16) but Peter was standing outside at the gate. So the other disciple, who was known to the high priest, went out, spoke to the woman who guarded the gate, and brought Peter in.
(17) The woman said to Peter, "You are not also one of this man's disciples, are you?"
He said, "I am not."
(18) Now the slaves and the police had made a charcoal fire because it was cold, and they were standing around it and warming themselves. Peter also was standing with them and warming himself.
(19) Then the high priest questioned Jesus about his teaching. (20) Jesus answered, "I

have always taught in the temple, where all come together. (21) Why do you ask me?"

(22) When he had said this, one of the police standing nearby struck Jesus on the face, saying, "Is that how you answer the high priest?"

(24) Then Annas sent him bound to Caiaphas the high priest. (25) They asked him, "You are not also one of his disciples, are you?"

He denied it and said, "I am not."

(26) One of the slaves of the high priest, a relative of the man whose ear Peter had cut off, asked, "Did I not see you in the garden with him?"

(27) Again Peter denied it, and at that moment the cock crowed.

(28) Then they took Jesus from Caiaphas to Pilate's headquarters. It was early in the morning. (29) Pilate said, "What accusation do you bring against this man?"

(33) Then Pilate summoned Jesus and asked him, "Are you the King of the

Jews?"

Jesus answered, "You say that I am a king."

(38) He told them, "I find no case against him. (39) But you have a custom that I release someone for you at the Passover. Do you want me to release for you the King of the Jews?"

(40) They shouted in reply, "Not this man, but Barabbas!" Now Barabbas was a bandit.

John 19

(1) Then Pilate took Jesus and had him flogged. (2) And the soldiers wove a crown of thorns and put it on his head, and they dressed him in a purple robe. (3) They kept coming up to him, saying, "Hail, King of the Jews!" and striking him on the face.

(6) And the police saw him, they shouted, "Crucify him! Crucify him!"

Pilate said to them, "I find no case against him."

(13) Pilate brought Jesus outside and sat on the judge's bench at a place called The Stone Pavement, or in Hebrew Gabbatha. (14) Now it was the day of Preparation; and it was about noon. (16) Then he

handed him over to them to be crucified.

So they took Jesus. (17) He went out to what is called The Place of the Skull, which in Hebrew is called Golgotha. (18) There they crucified him, and with him two others, one on either side. (19) *And there was written,* "Jesus of Nazareth, the King of the Jews." (20) And it was written in Hebrew, in Latin, and in Greek.
(23) When the soldiers had crucified Jesus, they took his clothes and divided them into four parts, one for each soldier. They also took his tunic; now the tunic was seamless, woven in one piece from the top. (24) So they said to one another, "Let us not tear it, but cast lots for it to see who will get it." This was to fulfill what the scripture says, "They divided my clothes among themselves, and for my clothing they cast lots."
(25) And that is what the soldiers did. Meanwhile, standing near the cross of Jesus were his mother, and his mother's sister, Mary the wife of Clopas, and Mary Magdalene. (28) After this, he said (in

order to fulfill the scripture), "I am thirsty."

(29) A jar full of sour wine was standing there. So they put a sponge full of the wine on a branch of hyssop and held it to his mouth.

(30) When Jesus had received the wine, he said, "It is finished." Then he bowed his head and gave up his spirit.

(31) Since it was the day of Preparation, the Jews did not want the bodies left on the cross during the sabbath. So they asked Pilate to have the legs of the crucified men broken and the bodies removed. (32) Then the soldiers came and broke the legs of the first and of the other who had been crucified with him. (33) But when they came to Jesus and saw that he was already dead, they did not break his legs. (34) Instead, one of the soldiers pierced his side with a spear, and at once blood and water came out. (36) These things occurred so that the scripture might be fulfilled, "None of his bones shall be broken."

(37) And again another passage of scripture says, "They will look on the one

whom they have pierced." (38) After these things, Joseph of Arimathea, who was a disciple of Jesus, asked Pilate to let him take away the body of Jesus. Pilate gave him permission; so he came and removed his body and wrapped it with the spices in linen cloths.

(41) Now there was a garden in the place where he was crucified, and in the garden there was a new tomb in which no one had ever been laid. (42) And so, because it was the day of Preparation, and the tomb was nearby, they laid Jesus there.

John 20

(1) Early on the first day of the week, Mary Magdalene came to the tomb and saw that the stone had been removed from the tomb. (2) So she ran and went to Simon Peter and said, "They have taken the Lord out of the tomb, and we do not know where they have laid him."
(3) Then Peter set out and went toward the tomb and went into the tomb. (9) For as yet they did not understand the scripture, that he must rise from the dead. (10) Then *he* returned to *his* home.

(11) But Mary stood weeping outside the tomb. As she wept, she bent over to look into the tomb; (12) and she saw two angels in white, sitting where the body of Jesus had been lying, one at the head and the other at the feet. (14) She turned around and saw Jesus standing there. (15) Jesus said to her, "Whom are you looking for, Mary?"
She said to him in Hebrew, "Rabbouni!."
(17) Jesus said to her, "Do not hold on to me. But go to my brothers."
(18) Mary Magdalene went and announced to the disciples, "I have seen the Lord."
(19) When it was evening on that day and the doors of the house where the disciples had met were locked, Jesus came and stood among them and said, "Peace be with you." (20) He showed them his hands and his side. Then the disciples rejoiced when they saw the Lord.
(22) He breathed on them and said to them, "Receive the Holy Spirit."
(30) Now Jesus did many other signs in the presence of his disciples, which are not written in this book. (31) But these are

written so that you may come to believe
that Jesus is the Messiah, the Son of God.

Conclusion

Let us first state an obvious but often missed fact – None of the Gospels claim authorship. Nowhere in the Gospels are we told who the authors were. Names assigned to the gospels were done so after the fact, by the church, according to tradition, as a way of labeling the books. The books were simply given those titles. The Gospels have no signature of authorship. As a reminder, let us look at the opening statements of each gospel. In them we will find no statement of authorship.

Mark 1
1 The beginning of the good news about Jesus the Messiah, the Son of God

Matthew 1
1 This is the genealogy of Jesus the Messiah the son of David, the son of Abraham:

Luke 1
1 Many have undertaken to draw up an account of the things that have been fulfilled among us, 2 just as they were handed down to us by those who from the first were eyewitnesses and servants of the word.

John 1

1 In the beginning was the Word, and the Word was with God, and the Word was God. 2 He was with God in the beginning.

With the possible exception of Mark, there is little possibility that any of the gospels were written by the people whose names are attached to them as authors. Matthew, Luke, and John were probably not the authors of the books bearing their names. If they were they would not have had to use source materials. The fact that Matthew and Luke used Mark as a source may indicate they thought Mark was authentic, but it also proves they were not eyewitnesses and probably not the real Matthew or Luke. Since Mark admits to not being an eyewitness but instead being a scribe for Peter, we have at best a second hand account of events a decade or two past from a man whose memory was fading. The Gospels are not books written in a single sitting by a single person. They are collections of available information. Indeed, if we believe Mark used what was available from Q at the time, we are left wondering why an eyewitness used a list of sayings. Q1 was the only part of Q we are reasonably certain was available at the time and the only reliable repository of the sayings of Jesus. But that would only be needed if the writer did not remember or did not witness the events at all.

If everyone who wrote the gospels had written what he or she remembered the wording, events, and emphasis of each would have been markedly different. Instead, the three synoptic gospels are so much alike it leaves little doubt they used the same cheat sheets.

As it turns out, Mark may have actually borrowed from Paul, since the first letter to the Corinthian Church was written prior to the Gospel of Mark. It is only in the last part of Mark that we see the idea of the blood sacrifice, and it is connected to the Lord's Supper.

At this point we should examine the fact that the idea of the blood sacrifice appears at the end of the Gospel of Mark, and is propagated into Matthew and Luke. Here is how Mark puts it:

And as they were eating, he took bread, and after blessing it broke it and gave it to them, and said, "Take; this is my body." And he took a cup, and when he had given thanks he gave it to them, and they all drank of it. And he said to them, "This is my blood of the covenant, which is poured out for many" (Mark 14:22-24).

Mark was written around 65 to 100 A.D. with most scholars placing it at around 68 A.D. But Mark, like all the Gospels, is a collection of traditions available at the time. Mark, as it turns out, is echoing what Paul put forth in 1 Corinthians some twenty years earlier.

First Corinthians is one of the four letters of Paul which are universally accepted to be authentic. The letter is usually dated c. 54/55 A.D. Werner Georg Kummel states (Introduction to the New Testament, p. 275): "The genuineness of I Cor is not disputed: the letter is already clearly known in I Clem 37:5; 47:1-3; 49:5; Ign., Eph 16:1; 18:1; Rom 5:1; Phila 3:3." Chronologically, this may be the first mention of the blood sacrifice. Paul says he got the idea from "the Lord" and explains it this way:

For I received from the Lord what I also handed on to you, that the Lord Jesus on the night when he was betrayed took bread, and when he had given thanks, he broke it, and said, "This is my body which is [broken] for you. Do this in remembrance of me." In the same way also he took the cup, after supper, saying, "This cup is the new covenant in my blood. Do this, as often as you drink it, in remembrance of me" (1 Corinthians 11:23-25).

The verbal similarities between these two accounts are remarkable and cannot be discounted. Paul's version of the Last Supper in 1 Corinthians was written at least twenty years earlier than Mark's Gospel. The doctrine was not built into the new faith. The first generation of elders controlling the church after the death of Jesus were not teaching this doctrine. Paul plainly says it is his own idea. He states: "For I received from the Lord what I handed on to you." His language is clear. He did not say he received it from one of the apostles or he learned it in Jerusalem from James. He states he got it "from the Lord." Paul uses the same language to defend his revelation and his new beliefs and thus the actions that followed, some of which went contrary to the doctrines of James and the first apostles who actually lived with Jesus. He says he did not receive it from any man, nor was he taught it, but swears with an oath, "I received it through a revelation of Jesus Christ" (Galatians 1:11-12).

New King James Version (NKJV)

Galatians 1:11 But I make known to you, brethren, that the gospel which was preached by me is not according to man. 12 For I neither received it from man, nor was I taught it, but it came through the revelation of Jesus Christ.

This means the idea of the blood sacrifice and its relation to the Lord's Supper with bread and wine representing the Flesh and Blood of Jesus comes to us from Paul. Mark, being a collection of traditions, was echoing it from Paul and Paul alone. Prior to Paul the tradition and doctrine did not exist. Matthew and Luke picked up the teaching from Mark, who got it from Paul, who never met Jesus outside of metaphysical encounters in the desert. It would not be long until the idea of the virgin birth would follow. After all, if the exsanguination of one person was going to cover the sins of all mankind to come, that blood had to be pure and sinless, maybe even supernatural. Maybe even from God. Further. If God found a woman to impregnate that woman would have to be very special, thus the idea of Mary's immaculate conception would be raised.

Before the Gospels

Is there no eyewitness among any of the Gospel writers? No, not one. Our hope of knowing anything from witnesses close to Jesus come down, not to the gospels but to the sources from which they used to write the gospels.

Dating Q is difficult, since it continued to be expanded and revised. Q1 was likely written around 40 to 50 A.D. Additions continued until 80 A.D. This would seem to fit generally since Thomas was written around 50 to 70 A.D. The Passion Narrative was written between 30 to 60 A.D. The Signs Gospel was likely written between 50 and 70 A.D. This means the first written account comes from a time ten to twenty years after Jesus, at the absolute earliest.

It is possible, just possible, that the authors of these source documents may have actually been witnesses to the life of Jesus. However, there is no way of knowing. They could have collected stories, folklore, and sayings from others, who themselves could have heard stories told, or could have been blessed to touch the hem of his garment.

At best, our gospels are second and third hand accounts with redactions throughout. Yet, in the Q1 Gospel, The Passion Narrative, The Gospel of Thomas, and the Signs Gospel we come closest to the person, theology, and history of Jesus.

The Gospel of Thomas and Q1 are the earliest recorded and unaltered saying of Jesus. Q1 may have influenced the Gospel of

Mark. Q1, which was the earliest recorded sayings of Jesus could have been used as a source document for Mark. The entire Q document, Q1, Q2, and Q3, was used as the basis of Luke and Matthew's Gospels. If we look at Q1 we should be closer to the real words of Jesus, without redactions and additions. In Q1 we should be able to see his teachings. Keeping in mind Q1 was written about 10 to 20 years after the death of Jesus, what we are seeing is a collection of memorable quotes, but at least some of these could be first hand testimonies. The words are pulled from the Gospel of Luke.

The translation is by Wim van der Dugen. The (K) designation indicates inclusion in Kloppenborg's edition.

Q1
ca.50 A.D.

These are the words of Jesus.
Seeing the crowds he said to his disciples :
Luke 6:20-21 (K8)

1 "How fortunate are the poor ; they have the Kingdom of Elohim.
2 How fortunate the hungry ; they will be fed.
3 How fortunate those who weep ; they will laugh."

Luke 6:27-35 (K9)

Before the Gospels

4 "But to you who hear, I say : love your enemies, bless those who curse you, and pray for those who mistreat you.

5 If someone slaps you on the cheek, offer the other as well. If anyone grabs your coat, let him have your shirt as well.

6 Give to anyone who asks, and if someone takes away which is yours, do not ask to have it back.

7 As you want people to treat you, do the same to them.

8 For if you love those who love you, what credit is that to you ? Even tax collectors love those who love them, do they not ?

9 And if you embrace only your brothers, what credit is that to you. Doesn't everybody do that ?

10 And if you lend to those from whom you hope to receive, what credit is that to you ? For wrongdoers also lend to their kind because they expect to be repaid.

11 On the contrary, love your enemies, do good and lend without expecting anything in return. Your reward will be great, and you will be children of Elohim. For He makes His sun rise on the evil and on the good ; He sends rain on the just and on the unjust."

Luke 6:36-38 - Mt.7:1-2 (K10)

12 "Be merciful even as your Father is merciful.

13 Judge not, and you will not be judged.

14 For you will be judged with the standard you judge with."

Luke 6:39-40 (K11)

15 He gave them a parable : "Can the blind lead the blind ? Will they not both fall into a pit ?
16 A student is not above his teacher. It is enough for a student to be like his teacher."

Luke 6:41-42 (K12)

17 "How can you look for the splinter in your brother's eye, and not notice the stick in your own eye ?
18 How can you say to your brother : 'Brother, let me pull out the splinter in your eye', when you do not see the stick in your own eye? You hypocrite ! First take the stick from your own eye, and then you can see to remove the splinter that is in your brother's eye."

Luke 6:43-45 (K13)

19 "A good tree does not bear rotten fruit ; a rotten tree does not bear good fruit.
20 Are figs gathered from thorns, or grapes from thistles ? Every tree is known by its fruit.
21 The good man produces good things from his store of goods and treasures ; and the evil man evil things. For the mouth speaks from a full heart !"

Luke 6:46-49 (K14)

22 "And why do you call me 'Master, master', and do not do what I say ?

23 Everyone who hears my words and does them, I will show you to whom he is like.

24 He is like a man who built a house on a rock. The rain fell, a torrent broke against the house, and it did not fall, for it had a rock foundation.

25 But everyone who hears my words but does not do them, is like a man who built a house on sand. The rain came, the torrent broke against it, and it collapsed. The ruin of that house was great."

Luke 9:57-62 (K21)

26 When someone said to Him : "Master, I will follow you wherever you go."

27 Jesus answered : "Foxes have holes, and birds of the air have nests, but the Son of Man has nowhere to lay his head."

28 When another said : "Let me first go and bury my father."

29 Jesus said : "Leave the dead to bury their dead."

30 Yet another said : "I will follow you, Master, but first let me say farewell to my family."

31 Jesus said to him : "No one who puts his hand to the plow and then looks back is fit for the Kingdom of Elohim."

Luke 10:2-11 (K22)

32 He said : "The harvest is great, but the workers are few ; beg therefore the Master of the harvest to send out workers into His harvest.

33 Go your ways : look, I send you out as lambs among wolves.

34 Do not carry purse, or bag, or sandals, or staff ; and do not greet anyone on the road.

35 Whatever house you enter, say : 'Peace be to this house !'

36 And if a child of peace is there, your peace will rest on him ; if not, let your peace return to you.

37 And stay in the same house, eating and drinking whatever they provide, for the worker deserves his wages. Do not go from house to house.

38 And if you enter a town, and they receive you, eat what is set before you,

39 heal the sick there, and say to them : 'The Kingdom of Elohim has come near to you.'

40 But if you enter a town and they do not receive you, as you leave, shake the dust from your feet and say :

41 'Nevertheless, be sure of this, the Kingdom of Elohim has come to you.'"

Luke 11:2-4 (K27)

42 He said to them : "When you pray, say : 'Father, may your name be holy. May your rule take place.

43 Always give us our bread.

44 Forgive us our debts, for we ourselves forgive everyone that is indebted to us. And lead us away from a trying situation'." (Some have – Deliver us from the evil one.)

Luke 11:9-11 (K28)

45 "Ask and it will be given to you ; seek and you will find ; knock and the door will be opened for you.
46 For everyone who asks receives, and the one who seeks finds, and to the one who knocks the door will be opened.
47 What father of yours, if his son ask for a loaf of bread, will give him a stone ?
48 Or if he ask for a fish, will give him a snake ?
49 So, if you, although you are not good, know how to give good gifts to your children, how much more will the Father above give good things to those who ask Him ?"

Luke 12:2-3 (K35)

50 "For nothing is hidden that will not be made known, or secret that will not come to light.
51 What I tell you in the dark, speak in the light, and what you hear as a whisper, proclaim on the housetops."

Luke 12:4 & 12:6-7 (K36)

52 "I say to you my friends : be not afraid of those that kill the body, and after that have nothing more to do.

53 Are five sparrows not sold for two cents ? Yet Elohim does not forget one of them.

54 Even the hairs of your head are all numbered. So don't be afraid. You are worth more than many sparrows."

Luke 12:13-21 (K40)

55 Someone from the crowd said to him : "Teacher, tell my brother to divide the inheritance with me."

56 He said to him : "Man, who made me your judge or divider ?"

57 He told them a parable, saying : "The land of a certain rich man produced in abundance.

58 And he thought to himself, saying : 'What should I do, for I have nowhere to store my crops ?'

59 And he said : 'This will I do. I will pull down my barns, and build larger ones, and there I will store all my wheat and my goods,

60 and I will say to my soul : Soul, you have ample goods stored up for many years. Take it easy, eat, drink, and be merry.'

61 But Elohim said to him : 'Foolish man ! This very night you will have to give back your soul. The things you produced, whose will they be ?'

62 That is what happens to he who stores up treasure for himself and is not rich in the sight of Elohim."

Luke 12:22-31 (K41)

63 And he said to his disciples : "I am telling you : do not worry about your life, what you will eat, or about your body, what you will wear.
64 Life is more than food, and the body is more than clothing.
65 Consider the ravens : they do not sow nor reap, they have neither storehouse nor barn, and Elohim feeds them. How much more are you worth than the birds ?
66 Which one of you can add a single day to his life by worrying ?
67 Consider the lilies how they grow : they toil not, they spin not. Yet I say to you, that Solomon in all his splendor was not arrayed like one of these.
68 If then Elohim so clothes the grass that is in the field today and thrown into the oven tomorrow, won't He put clothes on you, faint hearts ?
69 And you, seek not what you will eat or what you will drink, neither be disquieted.
70 For those of the world seek these things, and your Father knows that you need these things.
71 But rather seek the Kingdom of Elohim, and all these things will be yours as well.

Luke 12:33-34 (K42)

72 "Sell your possessions and give alms. Store up a treasure in the heavens for yourselves, where no thief can break in and steal and no moth consumes.

73 For where your treasure is, there your heart will also be."

Luke 13:18-21 (K49)

74 He said : "What is the Kingdom of Elohim like ? To what should I compare it ?
75 It is like a grain of mustard which a man took and sowed in his garden, it grew, became a great tree, and the birds of the air made nests in its branches."
76 He also said : "The Kingdom of Elohim is like yeast, which a woman took and hid in three measures of flour, till the whole was leavened."

Luke 14:11 (K54)

77 "He who glorifies himself will be humiliated, and he who humbles himself will be praised."

Luke 14:16-22 (K55)

78 "A man once gave a great supper, and invited many.
79 At the time of the banquet he sent his servant to say to those who had been invited : 'Come, for everything is now ready.'
80 But they all began to make excuses. The first said to him : 'I have bought a piece of ground, and I must go and see it. Please excuse me.'

Before the Gospels

81 And another said : 'I have bought five pair of oxen and I need to check them out. Please excuse me.'

82 And another said : 'I have married a woman and so I can't come.'

83 When the servant came home he reported this to his master. Then the master of the house in anger said to his servant : 'Go out quickly to the streets of the town and bring in as many people as you find.

84 And the servant went out into the streets and brought together everybody he could find.

85 That way the house was filled with guests.'"

Luke 14:26-27 & 17:33 (K56)

86 "Whoever does not hate his father and mother will not be able to learn from me.

Whoever does not hate his son and daughter cannot belong to my school.

87 Whoever does not bear his cross and just follows me, cannot be one of my disciples.

88 Whoever seeks to save his life will lose it ; but whoever loses his life on account of me will preserve it."

Luke 14:34-35 (K57)

89 "Salt is good : but if salt loses its taste, how to restore it ?

90 It is not good for either the land or the dunghill : people just throw it out.

91 Whoever has ears to hear, let him hear !"
(End Q1)

The teachings that set the world ablaze, when broken down, are childishly simple, yet impossibly difficult to perform. Jesus made them very plain. Religion clouded the issue. Jesus preached an inclusive gospel. Religion made this gospel exclusive, for the sake of control.

How much more simple could his teachings be? How much more difficult can they be to perform all the time, every day? But if they were put to use the world would change over night.

Seek to know God's love
Seek to show love and mercy.
Do not judge.
Do not do anything to others you would not want done to you.
Help the poor.
Pray for the sick.
Don't worry about the future or material possessions.
Fully commit to this way of life.
Expect that when you do people will not like you because you will be different.
Do not fear death. God awaits his children.
Do not fear life. God's kingdom is near.
Do these things. The rest is commentary.

Appendix

Dating Ancient Manuscripts?

Scholars use a number of methods to establish the date of manuscripts. Contrary to what some think, Carbon-14 dating is only accurate within a fifty to one-hundred year period on items of recent history. The older the object the wider the possible dating error, because error rates are calculated in percentage. Since Carbon-14 dating needs material from the item it necessitates the destruction of part of the item for sampling. For ancient papyrus or vellum or other very precious material this may not be possible. For this reason, generally more indirect methods of dating are used.

Perspectives change in time. One way to set a date is to look at events mentioned in the text. If some event is mentioned or described the text must have been written after the date of occurrence. What is said about an occurrence could also help date and place the author. The recent wars in the Middle East, the first one ending in 1991 and the second continuing at the writing of this chapter, was thought to be a good idea, but after the U.S. went on to free Afghanistan it was understood by most that the actions unleashed a backlash of resistance and terrorism, which has called into question the wisdom of either war. Distance in time clarifies events.

Language and word choices are other indicators of date. Let us take a few recent examples. The words "transistor, computer, and data are recent occurrences. We know that computers have only been around as home appliances since the late 1980's. Floppy drives have already come and gone. Words come into style and go out in a matter of a generation. We no longer use the words snazzy, hep, or groovy. Use of these words would date the writing to within just a few years. Languages change and morph. Ours does, and so does any language in constant use. This simple idea can be clouded when manuscripts are added to and changed over time as words and ideas outside the original timeframe are introduced to older writings.

Writing styles change. The way letters are formed change over period of time. *from one script or style to another script, or to another style,* scripts change over time. Even the alphabet itself changes. The letter "W" was not used before the 7th century A.D. and did not see common use until the 11th century A.D.

The letter 'J' emerged in Middle High German. Gian Giorgio Trissino (1478-1550) was the first to explicitly distinguish I and J as representing separate sounds, in Trissino's epistle about the letters recently added in the Italian language" of 1524.

Even the way sentences and paragraphs are written change over time. The ancient Greeks did not have any equivalent to our modern devices of punctuation. Punctuation was invented several centuries after the time of Christ. The oldest copies of both the Greek New Testament and the Hebrew Old Testament were written with no punctuation at all. The ancient Greeks used no spaces between words or paragraphs. Texts were a continuous string of letters, without spaces or punctuation. Early Greeks had only one case of letters. Texts were written in what we would think of as all capitals.

The writing instruments and mediums are indicators of general timeframes in which the production of a document occurred. Papyrus was first manufactured in Egypt and Southern Sudan as far back as the fourth millennium BC. The earliest archaeological evidence of papyrus was excavated in 2012-2013 at Wadi al-Jarf, an ancient Egyptian harbor located on the Red Sea coast. These documents date from ca. 2560-2550 BC (end of the reign of Khufu).

Between 100 B.C. to 100 A.D. parchment began to rival papyrus. Parchment was prepared from animal skins. Sheets of parchment were folded to form quires from which book-form codices were fashioned. Early Christian writers soon adopted the codex form, and in the Græco-Roman world, it became common to cut sheets from papyrus rolls to form codices. The latest certain dates for the use of papyrus are 1057 for a papal decree (typically conservative, all papal bulls were on papyrus until 1022), under Pope Victor II, and 1087 for an Arabic document. Its use in Egypt continued until it was replaced by more inexpensive paper introduced by Arabs.

Papyrus was replaced in Europe by the cheaper parchment and vellum, of significantly higher durability in moist climates.

The term parchment is a general term for an animal skin which has been prepared for writing or printing. Parchment has been made for centuries, and is usually calf, goat, or sheep skin. The term vellum from the French veau refers to a parchment made from calf skin.

By examining the materials used to produce the manuscript, such as the ink and parchment, scholars can start with a general span of time. Then by looking at the letters, style of script, use of word choices, and sentence structures scholars continue to narrow the dating possibility. The content and occurrences written about in the text puts the finishing boundaries on the document's date.

Although there are many other considerations, these are the main items examined when dating a codex.

It is easy to see how controversies could exist between scholars when it comes to placing dates on ancient writings.

www.ingramcontent.com/pod-product-compliance
Lightning Source LLC
Chambersburg PA
CBHW071659090426
42738CB00009B/1593